THE ART OF CHINESE POETRY

THE ART OF
CHINESE POETRY

JAMES J. Y. LIU

THE UNIVERSITY OF CHICAGO PRESS

CHICAGO AND LONDON

To Claire

Midway reprint 1983
Printed in the United States of America

ISBN: 0–226–48685–0
LCN: 62–7475

CONTENTS

Contents

Contents

Imagery involving puns—Differences between earlier and later poetry in the use of imagery—Criteria for imagery—How to use borrowed imagery—Imagery in dramatic poetry—Fossilized imagery—Imagery as revelation of poet's personality—Symbols: conventional and personal—Symbolism distinguished from allegory—Symbolism combined with imagery—Criteria for symbolism—Modification of conventional symbols by different poets

General and specific allusions—Purposes of allusions in poetry—Allusions in dramatic poetry—Allusions combined with imagery and symbolism—Quotations in poetry, especially poetic drama—Derivations and the question of originality

Natural tendency towards antithesis in Chinese—Antithesis distinguished from 'parallelism'—Antithesis in early Chinese poetry—In Regulated Verse—In Lyric and Dramatic Metres

INTRODUCTION

I n recent years, a fair amount of Chinese poetry has been translated into English, and there have even been a few English biographies of individual Chinese poets, but little has been written in English in the way of criticism. This is not surprising in view of the obvious difficulties of criticizing poetry in a language far removed from the one in which it is written. Nevertheless, the English-speaking reader who has acquired some knowledge of and taste for Chinese poetry through translations might well wonder at times: How should one approach Chinese poetry critically? Could one apply to it the technique of verbal analysis now prevailing in English and American literary criticism? What critical standards did Chinese critics in the past adopt? And what does Chinese poetry sound like? What are the principles of versification and the major verse forms and poetic devices? Difficult as some of these questions admittedly are, the fact that most English-speaking readers interested in Chinese poetry, of whom there appear to be quite a few apart from professional sinologues, cannot devote years to the study of the Chinese language, seems to justify an attempt, quixotic perhaps, but much needed, to answer them, if only partially and tentatively.

Since no serious criticism of poetry is possible without discussing various aspects of language, no more than serious criticism of painting is possible without discussing colour, line, and form, our enquiry must begin with a consideration of the Chinese language as a medium of poetic expression, as compared with English. We have to become aware of the similarities, and even more of the differences, between the two languages, and beware of the dangers of misapprehension that may ensue from the latter. Differences between Chinese and English exist on several levels. First of all, some differences lie in the nature of the two languages themselves, such as phonetic and grammatical ones. Then there are differences due to unique concepts or divergent ways of thinking and modes of feeling. For instance, there are no exact Chinese equivalents for 'humour' and 'snobbery', for the concepts expressed by these words do not exist in the Chinese mind. This is not to say that the Chinese have no sense of humour and are entirely free from snobbery, only that their conceptions of these are not identical with the English ones. On the other hand, such a Chinese concept as *hsiao*, usually inadequately translated as 'filial piety',[1] has no precise counterpart in English thinking, and hence no English word for it. Again, differences may arise out of dissimilar social and cultural environments or even physical objects. An English 'gentleman' is not exactly the same as a Chinese *chün-tzŭ*; the word 'house' conjures up a mental picture very different from that evoked by the Chinese word *fang*, which is usually taken as its equivalent. Such differences are inevitable, for after all language is a reflection of the mentality and culture of a people, and it in turn influences the way of thinking and cultural characteristics of the people who speak it as their mother tongue. In our discussions on the Chinese language as a poetic medium in Part I, differences between Chinese and English will be constantly borne in mind.

Meanwhile, honesty compels me to clarify my own position as an interpreter of Chinese poetry to English-speaking readers (for interpretation is the first part of a critic's task). The fact that I am writing in English for non-specialist readers will necessitate a great deal of translation, yet problems of translation will arise out of the very differences between the two languages that I shall be discussing. I shall thus find myself in the paradoxical position of having to find *ad hoc* solutions to certain problems in the process of discussing them or even before I can start to discuss them. This, however, will have its own reward: though we shall be primarily concerned with such differences only in so far as they affect poetic purpose and effect, our discussions cannot help being to some extent discussions on problems of translation at the same time, and would therefore possess not merely a theoretical interest but some practical value as well.

[1] see below, p. 10.

Introduction

Of course, criticism should go beyond an examination of language. Such basic questions as what poetry is or should be and how one should write poetry are bound to arise sooner or later. In Part II, I shall attempt to demonstrate how Chinese critics of the past would have answered these questions, thereby providing our own enquiry with a traditional background.

In Part III, I shall endeavour to achieve a synthesis among various schools of Chinese criticism and evolve a view of my own, from which critical standards for Chinese poetry can be derived. In applying these standards, I shall attempt a further synthesis— one between this mainly traditional Chinese view of poetry and the modern Western technique of verbal analysis. Naturally Chinese critics have carried out analyses of a sort, but they have usually been content with drawing attention to the felicity or clumsiness of particular words and phrases, seldom trying to probe into unconscious associations of ideas or to analyse systematically and critically the use of imagery and symbolism. Our own analysis of various poetic devices will be undertaken with a view to critical evaluation, for we should not forget that verbal analysis is after all a means and not an end, and that no analysis, however subtle and ingenious, is justified unless it deepens our understanding of poetry or makes us aware of the nature of our response to it.

From the above remarks it will be seen that Part I of this book consists mainly of information, Part II of interpretation, and Part III of criticism. Such being the case, the first part, intended to give the general reader the amount of knowledge about the Chinese language and Chinese versification needed to follow the critical discussions in the later parts, may prove rather dull reading. The reader is therefore asked to be patient while reading Part I, or, if he has no taste for linguistic discussions, start with Part II and only turn back to Part I when the need for information on specific points arises. The analytical table of contents, together with cross-references, should enable him to do so.

Throughout the book, examples of Chinese poetry are chosen from works ranging in time from about 600 B.C. to about A.D. 1350. Poems in traditional forms written since the latter date have been largely imitative and seldom of prime importance. As for poetry in modern colloquial Chinese, since it is in the main a deliberate attempt to break away from tradition and in many cases influenced by Western poetry, it requires no special interpretation to Western readers and is not discussed in this book.

Some Chinese characters are given in the text, either to illustrate the nature of the Chinese script, or simply to show what a poem looks like in the original. Furthermore, though this book is chiefly intended for the general reader, students of Chinese literature may also find it useful, and it is partly for them that the Chinese characters are included. For their further convenience, I have provided a list of references and an index of Chinese names and book titles.

Finally, a few words about my translations of poems in this volume. Since they are primarily meant to illustrate various aspects of poetic language, they have to be as close to the original as possible, though I have tried to make them readable as well. Where possible, I have followed the original verse form and rime scheme, and my reasons for doing so will be found on p. 21. I am aware of the uneven quality of my translations, but the inferior nature of some of them is due to the necessity of being literal or using an awkward expression, in order to show some particular feature of the original language or versification.

A FEW of the translations of Chinese poems in this volume have been published in *Oriental Art* (Oxford, 1951) and *The Adelphi* (London, 1953), while some of the material in Part II and Part III, Chapter 1, has previously appeared in articles in the *Journal of Oriental Studies* (Hong Kong University, 1956) and the *Proceedings of the XXIVth International Congress of Orientalists* (Munich, 1957). I am indebted to the editors and publishers concerned for permission to reprint these.

I am grateful to the Yale-in-China Association, New Haven, Conn., U.S.A., for a grant towards the cost of printing the Chinese characters in this book.

J. J. Y. L.

PART I

The Chinese Language as a Medium
of Poetic Expression

THE STRUCTURE OF CHINESE CHARACTERS

I T is generally realized that Chinese is written with characters instead of an alphabet—a feature which is the ultimate source of many of the characteristics of Chinese poetry. However, there is a fallacy still common among Western readers outside sinological circles, namely, that *all* Chinese characters are pictograms or ideograms. This fallacy on the part of some Western enthusiasts for Chinese poetry has had some curious results. Ernest Fenollosa in his essay, 'The Chinese Character as a Medium for Poetry', stressed this misconception and admired Chinese characters for their alleged pictorial qualities. While one can understand his enthusiasm for a language that he imagined to be free from the tendencies towards jejune logicality of modern English, and while one is flattered by his attribution of superior poetic qualities to one's mother tongue, one has to admit that his conclusions are often incorrect, largely due to his refusal to recognize the phonetic element of Chinese characters. Yet this essay, through Ezra Pound, has exerted considerable influence on some English and American poets and critics. This may be a happy example of the so-called catalytic effect of scholarship, but as an introduction to Chinese poetry, the Fenollosa approach is, to say the least, seriously misleading.

To clear away this basic misconception, we have to examine the principles underlying the structure of the characters. Traditional Chinese etymology postulates six principles known as the Liu

Shu. This term has been translated as 'The Six Scripts', though in fact it does not refer to six *classes* of characters but six *principles* regarding the formation of characters, and may therefore be rendered 'The Six Graphic Principles'. The definition and correct order of the six principles have been subjects of controversy among Chinese scholars for centuries, and we cannot enter here into intricate arguments about them. I shall simply describe each principle in the way that seems to me to be most reasonable, without quoting sources and authorities to support my interpretations. If any sinologue should object to this, I can only forestall his objection by pointing out that I am writing on Chinese poetry for a non-specialist public, not on Chinese philology for experts.

The First Graphic Principle is *Hsiang-hsing* 象 形, or 'Imitating the Form'. For instance, the character for *jih* ('sun') is 日 (ancient form ☉); that for *yueh* ('moon') is 月 (ancient form 𝔻); that for *jen* ('person') is 人 (ancient form 𝒥); that for *mu* ('tree') is 木 (ancient form 𝕏); that for *yang* ('sheep') is 羊 (ancient form 𝒴). These characters based on the First Principle may be called Simple Pictograms and represented by the letter P.

The Second Graphic Principle is *Chih-shih* 指 事, or 'Pointing at the Thing'. Characters based on this principle are symbols of abstract notions, not pictures of concrete objects. For example, the numbers *yi, erh, san* ('one, two, three') are represented by corresponding numbers of strokes: 一, 二, 三. Such characters may be called Simple Ideograms and represented by the letter I. Sometimes a Simple Ideogram may consist of an already existing Simple Pictogram with an additional indicator, e.g. the character for 'tree' with a stroke across its top becomes the character for *mo* ('tree top'): 末 (ancient form 𝕏), and the same character with a stroke across its base becomes the character for *pen* ('tree root'): 本 (ancient form 𝕏). These characters may be represented by the formula $I = P + i$, where i means indicator.

The Third Principle is *Huei-yi* 會 意 or 'Understanding the Meaning'.[1] This concerns the combination of two or more simple characters to form a new character in such a way as to suggest the meaning of the new one. For instance, the character for *ming* ('bright') is 明 (ancient form 𝕠𝔻), which consists of a window and a moon (*not* sun and moon); the character for *nan* ('man') is 男

---

[1] This is the usual explanation, although I strongly suspect that *huei* here means 'join', and the whole phrase means 'joining the meanings'.

(ancient form 𤲦), which consists of 'field' and 'strength'. Such characters may be called Composite Ideograms and represented by the letter C. Each component part of a Composite Ideogram may be a Simple Pictogram, Simple Ideogram, or another Composite Ideogram, as the case may be. (C = P + P'; C = P + I; C = I + I'; C = C' + P; C = C' + C''.)

The Fourth Principle is *Hsieh-sheng* 諧 聲, or 'Harmonizing the Sound'. This refers to the use of one character as a component part of another to indicate the sound of the latter. When thus used it is known in English as a 'phonetic'. At the same time, the other part of the composite character, which signifies the meaning, is called the 'radical' or 'significant'. Thus, if we use the letter N to represent a Composite Phonogram, it usually consists of a phonetic (p) and a significant (s), while the phonetic and the significant in themselves could be Simple Pictograms, Simple Ideograms, Composite Ideograms, or other Composite Phonograms. (N = p + s; p = P, I, C, N'; s = P', I', C', N''.) Thus, the Composite Phonogram for *chung* ('loyalty') is 忠, which consists of a phonetic *chung* 中 and a significant *hsin* 心 ('heart'). The phonetic *chung* in itself means 'middle', and is a Simple Pictogram, showing a line cutting through the middle of a square: 中 (p = I); while the significant *hsin* 心 (ancient form 𡨄) is a Simple Pictogram of the heart, which here signifies that 'loyalty' has something to do with the heart (s = P). Occasionally we find a Composite Phonogram with one phonetic and more than one significant. For example, the character for *pao* (Archaic[1] pronunciation *pog*; 'treasure') is 寶, which consists of a phonetic *fo* 缶 (Archaic[1] pronunciation *piog*), and three significants: 'roof' 宀, 'jade' 王, and 'mother-of-pearl' 貝. (N = p + s + s' + s''.)

The Fifth Principle is *Chuan-chu* 轉 注, or 'Mutually Defining', which is concerned with the use of synonymous characters.

The Sixth Principle is *Chia-chieh* 假 借, or 'Borrowing', which concerns the loan of homophones.

It will be seen that the last two principles are concerned with the extended *use* of already existing characters and not with the *formation* of new ones. Thus in fact there are only four basic principles underlying the structure of the characters, and consequently four main categories of them: Simple Pictograms,

---

[1] Archaic Chinese is the term used by the Swedish sinologue Bernhard Karlgren for the language of early Chou (cir. 1100–600 B.C.).

Simple Ideograms, Composite Ideograms, and Composite Phonograms. The first two form only a small minority, but since they are the characters for the most common objects (e.g. sun, moon, tree) or the most essential concepts (e.g. number, above, below, middle), they tend to disguise the fact they are only a minority. The majority of Chinese characters belong to the last category and contain a phonetic element. Moreover, even those characters which were originally formed on a pictographic principle have lost much of their pictorial quality, and in their modern forms bear little resemblance to the objects they are supposed to depict. (A comparison of the ancient forms with the modern forms of the Simple Pictograms given above will prove this.) The fallacy of Fenollosa and his followers should now be evident.

Another popular fallacy about written Chinese is the confusion between 'word' and 'character', with the consequent fallacy that Chinese is a monosyllabic language. A 'word' in Chinese, as in any other language, is a unit of speech, which may be of one or more syllables, and hence written with one or more characters. A 'character' is a written symbol which corresponds to one syllable and may form one word or part of a word. Theoretically each character has a meaning, but in actual usage some characters do not occur independently but only together with other characters, e.g. *ying-wu* 鸚鵡 ('parrot'), *hsi-shuai* 蟋蟀 ('cricket'—the insect, not the game, of course!), *miao-t'iao*[1] 窈窕 ('graceful'), and *p'u-t'ao* 葡萄 ('grapes'). These are to all intents and purposes disyllabic *words*, each written with two characters. Words of more than two syllables are rare, except for transliterations of foreign words, e.g. Ah-mi-t'o Fo 阿彌陀佛 (Amitabha Buddha). Sometimes a character may either occur independently or together with another character to form a 'compound'. The character *hsien* 先 ('first') and the character *sheng* 生 ('to be born') can each occur by itself, but together they form a compound *hsien-sheng* ('sir, gentleman, teacher'). A disyllabic *compound* differs from a disyllabic *word* in that each constituent part of a compound can occur separately, though not necessarily in the same sense as in the compound. Usually the meaning of a compound is derived from those of its constituent parts, though this may not be obvious. The meanings of *hsien-sheng*, 'sir, gentleman, teacher', are derived from the literal

---

[1] Most dictionaries give *miao-t'iao* and *yao-t'iao* as alternative pronunciations of this word, though I have never heard any Chinese using the latter.

senses of *hsien* and *sheng*: 'first born', hence, senior, to be respected, etc. A special case must be made of compounds containing allusions, whose meanings differ from the literal senses of their constituent parts put together. For instance, *chih-hsüeh* 志學, literally 'wish to study', is an allusion to Confucius's remark, 'At fifteen I set my mind on studying', and the compound is therefore not to be taken literally but as a conventional way of saying 'fifteen years of age'. Such allusive compounds are numerous in Chinese and set a constant trap for the unwary.

2

IMPLICATIONS AND ASSOCIATIONS OF WORDS AND CHARACTERS

As in English, and to an even greater degree, a word in Chinese does not always have one clear-cut, fixed meaning, but often covers different meanings, some of which may be mutually exclusive. Take a simple example: *sheng*; this word, used as a verb, could mean: to live, to give birth to, to be born; as a noun: life, young man, student; as an adjective: alive, raw, strange, innate, natural, lively. The *embarras de choix* presented by such words in Chinese has been demonstrated by Professor I. A. Richards in his *Mencius on the Mind*, and may become a source of constant obscurity. While this may be a serious drawback in expository prose, it can be an advantage in poetry, for it makes possible the expression of thought and emotion with the greatest economy of words. The poet can compress several meanings into one word, and the reader has to choose the meaning that seems most likely to be uppermost in the poet's mind, as well as probable subsidiary meanings, while excluding irrelevant meanings of which the word is capable in other contexts. This of course also happens in English, but not, I believe, to the same extent as in Chinese. In this respect, Chinese is a better language for writing poetry. Comparing the language of poetry with that of prose, Professor William Empson remarked, 'The demands of metre allow the poet to say something which is not normal colloquial

English, so that the reader thinks of the various colloquial forms which are near to it, and puts them together; weighing their probabilities in proportion to their nearness. It is for such reasons as this that poetry can be more compact, while seeming to be less precise, than prose.'[1] We may add that it is for similar reasons that Chinese can be more compact, while seeming to be less precise, than English.

As the above example shows, some of the different possible meanings of a word may be mutually incompatible, while others may be coexistent at the same time, with one of them predominating. It seems to me that only when the choice between alternative meanings is in doubt do we get a genuine case of 'ambiguity'; when several meanings of a word are present simultaneously, to a greater or lesser extent, we may regard one of them as its predominant meaning, and the others as its 'implications'. Thus I am using the word 'ambiguity' in its ordinary sense, not to cover all the seven Empsonian types. In fact, Professor Empson himself seems to have adopted 'implications' in his *Structure of Complex Words* for certain cases he had called 'ambiguities' in his earlier book.

Also, I think we should distinguish 'implications' from 'associations'. An 'association' is something connected in our mind with a word, not part of its meaning or one of its possible meanings. For instance, 'table' is associated with 'dinner' but does not imply the latter, as it implies, for example, 'flat surface'. Only in phrases like 'table manners' does 'dinner' become an implication instead of an association, for it is now an essential part of the definition of the phrase, though not explicitly stated. It will be noticed that my use of the word 'association' differs from Professor Empson's: he regards only private fancies as associations, while I exclude all private fancies from our discussion as being too intractable, but only deal with associations which may be presumed to be common among most readers. How such common associations arise I shall endeavour to show later on.

In Chinese, further complications arise out of the use of characters, with implications and associations of their own. I shall first consider the implications and associations of words *qua* words, then those of characters, and describe the interaction between them.

To begin with the implications of words. As I have already

[1] *Seven Types of Ambiguity* (revised edition, 1947), p. 28.

observed, a word may possess a predominant meaning and several subsidiary ones as its implications at the same time. For instance, the word *hsiao*, commonly translated as 'filial piety', in fact covers a whole range of meanings: to love, obey, honour, serve, and look after, one's parents, without necessarily pulling a long face, as the English word 'piety' rather suggests. Any of these meanings may be the predominant one, according to the context. When we apply the word to someone, we may mean he never goes against his parents' wishes, or simply he takes good care of them, with the ideas of 'love, honour, respect' as implications. 'He is devoted to his parents' might be a passable translation. A similar case in English would be some word like 'gentleman', which means 'a man entitled to bear arms but not included in the nobility', but usually carries the ideas of 'honour, gallantry, courtesy' etc. as implications. If we borrow Professor Empson's symbols, we can write these words with implications as A/1, 2, 3, etc.: e.g. *hsiao* = love one's parent/honour, obey, etc.

I have used the word 'predominant' to designate the meaning that seems uppermost in the mind of the user in a particular context. I should like to point out that this 'predominant' meaning is not necessarily the same as the one the word was given at the time of its invention, which I shall call its 'original' meaning; nor is the 'predominant' meaning necessarily the same as the one in which the word is most frequently used, which I shall call its 'usual' meaning. For instance, the 'original' meaning of the word *mu* 木 is 'tree', but its 'usual' meaning in modern usage is 'wood', while its 'predominant' meaning is such compounds as *mu-no* 木訥 or *ma-mu* 麻木 is 'stiff'. The distinction between original, usual, and predominant meanings also exist in English, and we need only think of words like 'gentleman' and 'chamberlain' to realize this. In fact, what I call 'predominant' meaning is the same as Professor Empson's 'chief' meaning, and my 'original' and 'usual' meanings are both covered by what he calls 'head' meaning.[1] If anyone should doubt the necessity of pointing out such fine distinctions of meaning, I would answer that these distinctions, though generally taken for granted by native speakers of a language, may present real difficulties to foreign students of the language and to translators, and are for this reason alone worth discussing.

[1] *The Structure of Complex Words*, p. 38.

Sometimes, an implication, instead of adding subsidiary meanings to the predominant one, may further define or qualify it, thereby limiting its applicability rather than extending it. For example, the word *ch'i* 萋 ('flourishing') is only applied to grass. Thus, 'grass' becomes an implication of the word, and may be written in brackets after the meaning: *ch'i* = flourishing (grass). In English, we find similar cases with words like 'contrapuntal', which implies 'music'. This is a different case from 'Honest—of women: chaste' discussed by Professor Empson,[1] for a word like *ch'i* or 'contrapuntal' can only be legitimately applied to one object, whereas 'honest' can be applied to objects other than women, though in different senses. And if we do apply a word to things other than the one for which it is intended, it becomes a metaphor, as when we speak of 'contrapuntal prose'.

Next, let us consider the associations of words. There are several kinds, apart from those induced purely by personal fancy:

(1) Notional associations: those aroused by the object the word denotes (or its 'referent'), not by the sound, visual form, or etymology of the word itself. Such associations may be due to some common belief or custom, or due to some legend or myth. In Chinese poetry, the willow is often associated with parting because in T'ang times it was a custom to break a willow twig and present it to a departing friend. Such associations are closely connected with the use of conventional symbols, which I shall discuss in a later chapter (Part III, Chapter 2). This kind of association also occurs in English, e.g. the association of the moon with chastity because of its identification with the goddess Diana, or that of the mistletoe with Christmas.

(2) Auditory associations: those aroused by the sound of the word. All conscious and unconscious puns are based on them. For instance, in a poem by the T'ang poet Liu Yü-hsi, written in the style of a folk song, the poet puns on the word *ch'ing* 晴 ('sunny'), which has the same sound as the word *ch'ing* 情 ('love'):

> The sun comes out in the east; it rains in the west:
> You'll say it's not sunny (love), yet it is.

Sometimes a pun may not be intended by the poet, but the effect of a word can be enhanced if we associate it with another word or

[1] *The Structure of Complex Words*, p. 35.

compound connected with it in sound. In a love poem by another T'ang poet, Li Shang-yin, this line occurs:

> The candle will drip with tears until it turns to ashes grey.

What I have translated as 'ashes grey' is in fact one single word *huei* 灰, which can be used as a noun, 'ashes', or an adjective, 'grey'. I think here it has the predominant meaning 'ashes', with 'grey' as an implication (ashes/grey). Further, the compound *huei-hsin* 灰 心 ('ash-hearted') means 'despair', and I do not think it is just my fancy to link 'ashes' here with 'ash-hearted', because the poet is describing a hopeless passion.

Puns, intended or otherwise, based on auditory associations, of course also occur in English poetry, and no examples need be given here.

(3) Contextual associations: words connected in a reader's mind because of some familiar literary context, not because of any inherent relation between them. For instance, I think most Chinese readers will associate the word *miao-t'iao* ('graceful') with the words *shu nü* 淑 女 ('virtuous lady'), as they occur together in the very first song in *The Book of Poetry* (*Shih Ching*), the earliest known anthology of Chinese verse, just as English readers may easily associate the word 'multitudinous' with 'incarnadine' because of their familiar context, though there is no logical relation between the words themselves. This kind of association differs from the first kind in that the words are arbitrarily connected, not connected by some real or imagined relationship.

The above kinds of associations may be presumed to be common among readers with similar education, reading experience, and sensibility, though it is of course impossible to say whether such associations *will* inevitably occur, or to draw a hard and fast line between private fancies and common associations. However, a critic is within his rights to point out any such associations as may enrich the meaning of a word in a given context.

Just as the predominant meaning of a word may change from context to context, so may its implications and associations vary accordingly, to the extent that they may disappear altogether at times. The word *hsiao*, when applied to someone in mourning for one of his parents, need not carry its usual implications of 'love, obey, honour', etc. In fact the opposite may have been true, but one still calls someone who has lost one of his parents *hsiao-tzŭ* (literally 'devoted son'), in the same way as one speaks of someone's 'bereavement' even if he may not feel it to be one. In English, 'gentleman' (fascinating word!) may again furnish us with analogous examples. Consider the varying implications of this word in the following contexts: in 'gentleman's agreement', the implications are mainly moral; in 'Gentlemen prefer blondes', they are social; in 'gentleman's gentleman', the main implication of the first 'gentleman' is social standing and that of the second is superior manners; 'gentlemen' used as a euphemism for 'men's lavatory', though the motive behind such a usage is a snobbish one, is practically devoid of the usual implications of the word. To move on to a higher plane, when Shakespeare in the Prologue to *Henry V* wishes for 'a Muse of *fire*, that would ascend / The brightest heaven of invention', the main implication of 'fire' is its upward-going nature as one of the four elements, while its usual implication of 'burning', with its association of 'destruction', is irrelevant here. Even when Cleopatra says before her death, 'I am *fire* and air, my other element / I give to baser life', the implication of 'fire' is still its upward-going attribute as a noble element, in contrast to the 'baser' elements earth and water that would sink down, though a modern audience might easily assume that the implication of 'fire' is 'passion'. The same implication is present when Donne writes, '*Fire* for ever doth aspire / And makes all like itself, turns all to fire', and when Michael Drayton writes of Marlowe, 'his raptures were / All air and *fire*, which made his verses clere'.

In certain contexts, not only the implications and associations but even the meaning itself may be dissociated from a word. For convenience' sake I shall discuss this below, together with the dissociation of meaning from *characters*.

We can now proceed to consider the implications and associations of *characters*. In so far as a character represents a word or part of a word, its implications and associations will be the same as those of the word. Some of these, though by no means all, are indicated by the visual form of the character, or part of it. But in addition, a character may have its own implications due to its etymology. Such implications may or may not be relevant to the usual meaning or predominant meaning of the word, even though they were relevant to the original meaning when the character was first invented for the word. (It is safe to assume that *words* existed before *characters*: the ancient Chinese must have had words for sun, moon, man, etc., and then invented written charaters for them, not *vice versa* as some Chinese scholars suggested. This can be proved by the Sixth Graphic Principle—that of phonetic loans, for unless a word had already existed with a sound of its own, how could one have borrowed the character for it for another word which had the same sound?) There is another possibility: the implications may be still relevant to the meaning of the word but no longer form part of the meaning, and are thus reduced to the status of *associations*. Let us consider the four categories of characters one by one.

In the case of Simple Pictograms, the visual form of the character makes vivid the meaning of the word it represents, without adding further implications. However, the forms of the characters have changed much since they were first invented, and the forms in which characters are now written, and have been for the past two thousand years or so, are highly stylized and have lost a great deal of their original pictorial quality. For instance, the ancient form of *jih* ('sun') is ☉, while its modern form is 日; the ancient form of *shuei* ('water') is 𣱱. its modern form 水. The loss of visual appeal is obvious.

In the case of Simple Ideograms, if the character is a simple sign, no implications are added to the meaning. But if it consists of a Simple Pictogram with an indicator ($I = P + i$), implications may be involved. Such implications may be still fully retained in the usual meaning of the word, e.g. the character for *jen* ('knife-edge'): 刃, which consists of a Simple Pictogram for 'knife' with a dot pointing to its edge. It is obvious that 'knife' is an implication of 'knife-edge'. But sometimes etymological implications may cease to be relevant altogether. For instance, as we have seen, the character for *mo* (original meaning: 'tree top') is 末, which consists of the Simple Pictogram for 'tree' with a line across its top. But the usual meaning of the word is simply 'tip' or 'end', and can be applied to anything. The implication 'tree' thus becomes quite irrelevant. The same is true of the character for *pen* (original meaning: 'tree root'), which consists of 'tree' with a line across its bottom: 本. The usual meaning of the word is simply 'basis', without the implication of 'tree'. Such dissociation of implications from characters is comparable to the virtual disappearance of the original metaphorical implications from English words like 'root' or 'source'.

With Composite Ideograms, the etymological implications may be fully retained, partially lost, or totally lost. For instance, the character for *sen* ('of trees, luxuriant'), 森, consists of three 'trees', where the implication is fully retained. But when the same character is used to mean 'dark', the implication becomes merely an association. We may represent the second meaning thus: *sen* = dark → trees, where the arrow represents an association of ideas. Sometimes the implication may become entirely irrelevant, such as in the character for *chia* ('home'), which consists of a 'roof' with a 'pig' under it: 家 (ancient form 家). We may put a 'not equal to' mark (≠) before such a dissociated implication: *chia* = home (≠ pig under roof).

Paradoxically, while implications based on genuine etymology may become irrelevant, those based on pseudo-etymology can be relevant. For example, the character for *ming* ('bright') in its ancient form consists of a 'window' and a 'moon', but in its modern form it is written with a 'sun' and a 'moon'.[1] Most readers fail to realize the true etymology of the character and may associate it with sun and moon—an association quite relevant to its meaning.

With Composite Phonograms, the meaning of the part used as the significant can be fully retained as an implication, or reduced to the status of an association. To give two examples we have already seen, the character for *chung* ('loyalty') has the 'heart' significant; the character for *ch'i* ['flourishing (grass)'] has the 'grass' significant. In both cases the meaning of the significant is kept as an implication of the composite character. Sometimes implications may become only associations. For instance, in the character for *ts'ang* ('dark green'), 蒼, the 'grass' significant is only an association, for the colour does not necessarily imply 'grass', though it may suggest this. Similarly, in the disyllabic word *ch'i-ch'ü* 崎嶇 ('rugged'), both characters have the 'mountain' significant. Here, 'mountain' is not an implication of the usual meaning of the word, but forms a relevant association: *ch'i-ch'ü* = rugged —→ mountain. Another example is *wang-yang* 汪洋 ('vast'), which contains the 'water' significant. Since the compound is not applied to water only, 'water' here is an association rather than an implication: *wang-yang* = vast —→ water.

---

[1] See above, p. 4.

15

As may be expected, the part used as the phonetic in a Composite Phonogram is usually dissociated from its own meaning. Thus, 妻, the phonetic in *ch'i* 萋, is dissociated from its own meaning 'wife'; and 倉, the phonetic in *ts'ang* 蒼, from its own meaning 'granary'; 奇 and 區, the phonetics in *ch'i-ch'ü* 崎嶇, are dissociated from their own meanings 'strange' and 'district'; 王 and 羊, the phonetics in *wang-yang* 汪洋, from their meanings 'king' and 'sheep'. We may represent such phonograms thus: *ch'i* = flourishing (grass) = grass + *ch'i* (≠ wife); *ts'ang* = dark green —→ grass = grass + *ts'ang* (≠ granary); *ch'i-ch'ü* = rugged —→ mountain = [mountain + *ch'i* (≠ strange)] + [mountain + *ch'ü* (≠ district)]; *wang-yang* = vast —→ water = [water + *wang* (≠ king)] + [water + *yang* (≠ sheep)].

Complicated as this may look on paper, in fact the process of dissociation takes place quite simply in the mind of the reader. As soon as he realizes a character is being used as the phonetic of a Composite Phonogram, he automatically dissociates it from its original meaning, much in the same way as an English reader will dissociate from 'ladybird' and 'butterfly' the literal meanings of their component parts.

In rare cases, the meaning of the phonetic may be relevant to the meaning of the whole character. For instance, the phonetic of *chung* ('loyalty') is *chung* 中, which by itself means 'middle'. It would not be out of place to think of 'loyalty' as 'having one's heart in the middle', though this is etymologically unsound. Another example is *ch'ou* 愁 ('sorrow'), which has a phonetic *ch'iu* 秋 and a significant 'heart' 心. As autumn is regarded as a sad season in China, it would not be irrelevant to think of 'sorrow' as 'autumn-hearted'. However, such cases are rare, and one should not indulge in this kind of pseudo-etymology, no matter how poetic and interesting the result may seem to be.

Not only can meanings be dissociated from parts of a character, but they can be dissociated from whole characters representing different words. I have already suggested, in fact, that meanings may be dissociated from words, and as we are now concerned with characters used as words, there is no need to differentiate between the two in the present instance. There are several situations in which meaning may be dissociated from a word (or, the character which represents it):

(1) When a character is used as part of a compound, the meaning

of which is different from the sum total of its constituent parts. For instance, in the compound *t'ien-hua* 天花, which means 'small-pox', the characters *t'ien* ('heaven') and *hua* ('flower') lose their original meanings. Or take an allusive compound like *chih-hsüeh*, which, as I have pointed out once before, is a conventional way of saying 'fifteen years old' and does not mean 'wish to study' (p. 7). Such compounds may be written thus: *t'ien-hua* = small-pox (≠ heavenly flower); *chih-hsüeh* = fifteen years old (≠ wish to study). These are like idiomatic phrases in English such as 'red herring', 'brown study', or 'white elephant'. Sometimes the meaning of the individual character may be remotely connected with that of the compound, such as in *hsien-sheng* ('sir, gentleman, teacher'), where the meanings of *hsien* ('first') and *sheng* ('born') are still remotely connected with the whole compound. We may write such a compound like this: *hsien-sheng* = sir, gentleman, teacher ('first born'). Such words are like 'skyscraper', 'curtain-raiser', etc., in English.

(2) When a character is used for transliterating foreign words. It is obvious that when used for transliteration, characters lose their meanings. However, the meanings of the characters can easily remain as *associations*. That is probably why early Chinese translators of Sanskrit sutras deliberately chose uncommon characters with few, if any, associations of their own for transliteration, such as *nieh-p'an* 涅槃 for 'nirvana', where the two characters, meaning 'black mud' and 'plate' respectively, do not occur often elsewhere. On the other hand, a translator can introduce flattering associations by using characters with nice meanings, such as the usual transliteration for 'English', *ying-chi-li* 英吉利, literally 'heroic, lucky, profitable'.

(3) When characters are used as proper names. When used as a surname, the meaning of a character is dissociated from it. No one thinks of a man whose surname is Chang as 'Mr. Open' or one whose surname is Li as 'Mr. Plum', any more than one would think of Shakespeare as someone brandishing a weapon or Smith as someone beating iron. As for personal names in Chinese, they are made up for each occasion, unlike English Christian names which are chosen from a number of existing ones. Hence Chinese personal names are more meaningful. Nevertheless, as soon as one recognizes a name as such, one need no longer think of its literal meaning, which may bear no relation to the character of the person

so named. Thus, one need not be more conscious of the literal meaning of a Chinese name like, say, Shu-lan ('Virtuous Orchid') than one is of the literal meanings of English names like Rosemary, Hope, or Patience. It is therefore misleading to translate Chinese names, unless one is deliberately trying to cater for the taste of some English-speaking readers for quaint *chinoiserie* of the Lady Precious Stream variety. The same is true of place names. One need no more think of Shantung as 'East of the Mountain' than one would of Oxford as a river crossing for cattle. Dynastic names such as Ming ('Bright') and reign titles such as T'ien Pao ('Heavenly Treasure') are usually regarded as just designations of certain periods in history, largely dissociated from the meanings of the characters. Exceptions to the above observations occur when a play on words is intended, such as in satirical verse, where a name can be seized on as a vulnerable target.

(4) In conventional polite phrases. Words so used are not to be taken literally. For instance, *p'u* 僕 ('servant') and *ch'ieh* 妾 ('handmaid') were, for all practical purposes, simply conventional ways of saying 'I', and it would be wrong to attribute undue humility to the user, just as in English it would be misleading to take literally such phrases as 'Dear Sir' or 'Your obedient servant'.

From all that has been said above it should be clear now that the pictorial qualities and etymological associations of Chinese characters can be greatly exaggerated, as indeed they have been by Fenollosa, Pound, and Florence Ayscough. The typical method of these worthies is to split a character into several parts and explain its meaning according to its real or imagined etymology. Some of the absurd results of this method have been demonstrated in Professor William Hung's *Tu Fu: China's Greatest Poet* [1] and in Mr. Achilles Fang's article 'Fenollosa and Pound', [2] and no further examples are necessary. Suffice it to say that this split-character method is at best like insisting that one must always think of 'philosophy' and 'telephone' as, respectively, 'love of wisdom' and 'far sound'; and that at worst it is like explaining 'Hamlet' as meaning 'small ham' and 'Swansea' as 'la mer des cygnes'. While one has no wish to deny the additional aesthetic enjoyment afforded by the form of the characters in Chinese

[1] Harvard University Press, (1952).
[2] *Harvard Journal of Asiatic Studies*, Vol. XX, Nos. 1 and 2 (1957).

poetry, the fact remains that a line of poetry written in Chinese characters is not a mere sequence of images like a film in slow motion, as Fenollosa thought, but a highly complex organic development of sense and sound (like poetry in any other language), with not a little suggestion, but little more than a *suggestion*, of the visual aspect of what is being described.

3

AUDITORY EFFECTS OF
CHINESE AND THE BASES
OF VERSIFICATION

J UST as the visual effects of Chinese characters in poetry have
been exaggerated, so have the auditory effects of Chinese
poetry been relatively neglected by Western translators and
students. Admittedly, the music of poetry can never be fully re-
produced in translation, even with two related languages like, say,
French and Italian, let alone two widely different ones like
Chinese and English. Nevertheless, assuming that one inevitably
misses something in translation, it may be just as well to know
what one has missed. Reading a poem in translation is like look-
ing at a beautiful woman through a veil, or a landscape through a
mist, of varying degrees of thickness according to the trans-
lator's skill and faithfulness to the original; and while I do not
claim to possess the magic power of lifting the veil and dis-
persing the mist, I can at least point at the tantalizing features of
the beauty and the faint contours of the mountains. With this in
mind, I shall proceed to describe the most important and
characteristic auditory qualities of Chinese poetry and the bases of
versification, as applied to the major verse forms in Chinese. In
my translations of the poems given as examples below, I shall try
to keep as closely as possible to the original verse form, by giving
as many stresses in English as there are syllables in Chinese in each

line, and by following the original rime scheme.[1] I am not unaware
of the risks that riming entails, nor am I suggesting it is always
possible to follow the original rime scheme. Still, I think this is
worth attempting, if only to correct the impression among some
English-speaking readers that all Chinese poetry is written in a
kind of rimeless verse, an impression based on translations and
contrary to the truth. I realize that the use of rime in translations
of Chinese poetry is regarded as a sin in certain quarters, but it
seems to me unfair to the reader to tell him that a poem is written
in such and such a metre, with such and such a rime scheme, and
then give him a free verse translation. To draw an analogy with
European poetry, it is one thing to say that the *Divine Comedy* is in
terza rima; it is another to *produce* an English version in *terza
rima*, as Miss Dorothy Sayers and others have done.

Two characteristic auditory qualities of Chinese are the mono-
syllabic nature of the characters and their possession of fixed
'tones'. Whereas a *word* may consist of more than one syllable, as I
pointed out before (p. 6), a character is invariably monosyllabic.
Thus, in Chinese poetry, the number of syllables in each line is
identical with that of characters, and it is immaterial whether we
call a line a 'five-character line' or a 'five-syllabic line', though
personally I shall use the latter in discussing versification, as it
refers to the sound of the words, while the former refers to the
written forms. In a Chinese poem, the number of syllables in each
line naturally decides its basic rhythm. In some kinds of Chinese
verse, all the lines have the same number of syllables; in others,
the number varies, as we shall see below.

Next to the regularity or variation in the number of syllables,
variation in tone also plays an important part in Chinese versifica-
tion. Each syllable in Chinese is pronounced in a fixed tone. In
Classical Chinese, there are four tones: *p'ing* or 'Level', *shang* or
'Rising', *ch'ü* or 'Falling', and *ju* or 'Entering'. For metrical
purposes, the first tone is regarded as Level, while the other three
tones are regarded as Deflected (*tsê*). These tones differ from each
other not only in pitch but in length and movement. The first
tone is relatively long and keeps to the same pitch; the other three
are relatively short, and, as their respective names indicate, move
upward or downward in pitch, or stop suddenly. Thus, variation
in tone involves not only modulation in pitch but contrast be-

[1] Occasionally assonance will be used in lieu of rime.

tween long and short syllables. In the latter respect, Chinese verse resembles Latin quantitative verse, while the modulation in pitch plays a role in Chinese verse comparable to that of variation in stress in English verse. Variation in tone occurs in all Chinese verse: in early verse, there is no prescribed tone pattern, only natural modulation of tones; in later poetry, the tone pattern is fixed. (See below.)

Another important element of versification is rime. End-rime occurs in all Chinese verse. Other devices such as alliteration and onomatopoeia are also used occasionally. We can now proceed to see how the various elements of versification play their parts in different verse forms.

Four-syllabic Verse. This is the earliest verse form in Chinese. The poems in *The Book of Poetry* (cir. 12th–7th centuries B.C.) are for the most part in four-syllabic lines, with occasional lines of more or fewer syllables. The lines are usually in short stanzas, with fairly complicated rime schemes. The following example from *The Book of Poetry* is called 'The Gentle Maiden'. I shall first give the text in Chinese characters; then a transcription according to the modern Pekinese pronunciation, together with the Archaic[1] pronunciations of the riming syllables according to Professor Bernhard Karlgren's reconstruction, and accompanied by a word-for-word English version; finally a verse translation, using rime or assonance where rime is used in the original.

靜　女

靜　女　其　姝
俟　我　於　城　隅
愛　而　不　見
搔　首　踟　躕

靜　女　其　孌
貽　我　彤　管
彤　管　有　煒
說　懌　女　美

自　牧　歸　荑
洵　美　且　異
匪　女　之　為　美
美　人　之　貽

[1] See footnote on p. 5 and Appendix.

Auditory Effects of Chinese

Ching Nü
Gentle Girl

Ching nü ch'i shu (t'iu)
Gentle girl how beautiful
Ssŭ wo yü ch'eng yü (ngiu)
Await me at city corner-tower
Ai erh pu chien
Love but not see
Sao shou ch'ih-ch'u (d'iu)
Scratch head pace to-and-fro

Ching nü ch'i luan (bliwan)
Gentle girl how pretty
Yi wo t'ung kuan (kwan)
Give me red pipe
T'ung kuan yu wei (giw∂r)
Red pipe has brightness
Yueh-yi ju mei (mi∂r)
Delight your beauty

Tzŭ mu kuei t'i (di∂r)
From pasture send shoot
Hsün mei ch'ieh yi (gi∂g)
Truly beautiful and rare
Fei ju chih wei mei (mi∂r)
Not your being beautiful
Mei jen chih yi (di∂g)
Beautiful person's gift

The Gentle Maiden

How pretty is the gentle maiden!
At the tower of the city wall she should be waiting.
I love her but I cannot see her;
I scratch my head while anxiously pacing.

The gentle maiden: how lovely is she!
This red pipe she gave to me.
O red pipe, with lustre bright,
Your beauty gives me great delight.

From the pasture she sent me her plight—
A tender shoot, beautiful and rare.
Yet it's not your beauty that gives me delight,
But she who sent you, so true and fair!

As we are only concerned with verse form at present, I shall
withhold comment on this poem till a later chapter (Part III,

Chapter 2). For the time being, I shall merely point out the chief metrical features of the poem. As will be seen from the above text and transcription, the poem is mainly in four-syllabic lines, with an occasional extra syllable (in stanza 1, line 2, and stanza 3, line 3). The rime scheme is: AAOA, BBCC, CDCD.

Ancient Verse (*Ku-shih* 古 詩; Five-syllabic or seven-syllabic). Poems in lines of five or seven syllables came into being in the Han dynasty (206 B.C.–A.D. 219). Later, these poems written in lines of five or seven syllables, without a fixed tone pattern, came to be known as Ancient Verse, in contrast to the Regulated Verse to be described below. In Ancient Verse, the number of lines in a poem is indefinite, but the number of syllables in each line is limited to five or seven, though occasional liberty is allowed. Rime usually occurs at the end of the even numbered lines, and one can either use one rime throughout or change the rime as one wishes. The following example is a five-syllable poem by Li Po (A.D. 701–762). The transcription is given according to the modern Pekinese pronunciation, with the riming syllables also in Karlgren's reconstructed pronunciation of Ancient Chinese.[1]

月 下 獨 酌

花 間 一 壺 酒
獨 酌 無 相 親
舉 杯 邀 明 月
對 影 成 三 人
月 既 不 解 飲
影 徒 隨 我 身
暫 伴 月 將 影
行 樂 須 及 春
我 歌 月 徘 徊
我 舞 影 零 亂
醒 時 同 交 歡
醉 後 各 分 散
永 結 無 情 遊
相 期 邈 雲 漢

[1] This refers to Chinese of cir. A.D. 600. Cf. footnote on p. 5 and Appendix.

Auditory Effects of Chinese

Yueh Hsia Tu Cho
Moon-beneath Alone Drink

Hua chien yi hu chiu
Flowers-among one pot wine
Tu cho wu hsiang ch'in (ts'ien)
Alone drink no mutual dear
Chü pei yueh ming yueh
Lift cup invite bright moon
Tuei ying ch'eng san jen (nzien)
Face shadow become three men
Yueh chi pu chieh yin
Moon not-only not understand drink
Ying t'u suei wo shen (sien)
Shadow in-vain follow my body
Chan pan yueh chiang ying
Temporarily accompany moon with shadow
Hsing lo hsü chi ch'un (ts'iuen)
Practise pleasure must catch spring
Wo ko yueh p'ai-huai
I sing moon linger-to-and-fro
Wo wu ying ling luan (luan)
I dance shadow scatter disorderly
Hsing shih t'ung chiao huan
Wake time together exchange joy
Tsui hou ko fen san (san)
Rapt-after each separate disperse
Yung chieh wu-ch'ing yu
Always tie no-passion friendship
Hsiang ch'i miao yun-han (xan)
Mutual expect distant Cloud-river

Drinking Alone Beneath the Moon

A pot of wine before me amidst the flowers:
I drink alone—there's none to drink with me.
Lifting my cup to invite the brilliant moon,
I find that with my shadow we are three.
Though the moon does not know how to drink,
And my shadow in vain follows me,
Let me have their company for the moment,
For while it's spring one should be care-free.
As I sing, the moon lingers about;
As I dance, my shadow seems to fly.
When still sober we enjoy ourselves together;
When rapt with wine we bid each other good-bye.
Let us form a friendship free from passions
And meet again in yonder distant sky!

In the above poem two rimes are used, the first at the end of the 2nd, 4th, 6th, and 8th lines, the second at the end of the 10th, 12th, and 14th lines. The *yin* at the end of line 5 and the *huan* at the end of line 11 are *not* riming syllables, as they do not have the same kind of tone as the riming ones. The resemblance to a sonnet is a coincidence.

Regulated Verse (Lü-shih 律 詩; *Five- or seven-syllabic).* The Regulated Verse became an established verse form at the beginning of the T'ang dynasty (618–907). It was also known as the Modern Style *(chin t'i* 近 體) in contrast to the Ancient Verse, also called Ancient Style *(ku t'i* 古 體). The metrical rules of Regulated Verse are as follows:

(1) A poem should consist of eight lines.

(2) The lines must be either all five-syllabic or all seven-syllabic.

(3) The same rime is used throughout a poem. In a five-syllabic poem, rime is used at the end of the 2nd, 4th, 6th, and 8th lines; riming at the end of the first line being optional. In a seven-syllabic poem, rime occurs at the end of the 1st, 2nd, 4th, 6th, and 8th lines; that at the end of the 1st line being omitted sometimes.

(4) The four lines in the middle must form two antithetical couplets (cf. Part III, Chapter 4).

(5) There is a fixed tone pattern, though some liberty is allowed to syllables occupying less important positions (usually the 1st and 3rd syllables in a five-syllabic line; the 1st, 3rd, and 5th syllables in a seven-syllabic line). The standard tone patterns are given below: (— represents a Level Tone, + represents a Deflected Tone, / represents a pause, R represents a rime).

Five-syllabic Regulated Verse, first form:

$$— — / — + + \text{ (or, } — — / + + — \text{ R, if rime is desired)}$$
$$+ + / + — — \text{ R}$$
$$+ + / — — +$$
$$— — / + + — \text{ R}$$
$$— — / — + +$$
$$+ + / + — — \text{ R}$$
$$+ + / — — +$$
$$— — / + + — \text{ R}$$

Five-syllabic Regulated Verse, second form:

$+ + / - - +$ (or, $+ + / + - -$ R, if rime is desired)
$- - / + + - R$
$- - / - + +$
$+ + / + - - R$
$+ + / - - +$
$- - / + + - R$
$- - / - + +$
$+ + / + - - R$

Seven-syllabic Regulated Verse, first form:

$- - / + + / + - - R$ (or, $- - / + + / - - +$, if rime is omitted)
$+ + / - - / + + - R$
$+ + / - - / - + +$
$- - / + + / + - - R$
$- - / + + / - - +$
$+ + / - - / + + - R$
$+ + / - - / - + +$
$- - / + + / + - - R$

Seven-syllabic Regulated Verse, second form:

$+ + / - - / + + - R$ (or, $+ + / - - / - + +$, if rime is omitted)
$- - / + + / + - - R$
$- - / + + / - - +$
$+ + / - - / + + - R$
$+ + / - - / - + +$
$- - / + + / + - - R$
$- - / + + / - - +$
$+ + / - - / + + - R$

From the above patterns one can clearly perceive the principles of variation of tones within the line, and repetition and contrast of tone-sequences in the whole poem. It is naturally impossible to convey the actual qualities of the tones on paper; however, if an English-speaking reader would read the patterns aloud, using the word 'long' for Level Tones while keeping at an even pitch, and 'short' for Deflected Tones while dropping the pitch a little, he would get a rough idea of the rhythm and tonal variations of Chinese Regulated Verse.

The following is an example of Seven-syllabic Regulated Verse by Li Shang-yin (813–858):

無　題

相　見　時　難　別　亦　難
東　風　無　力　百　花　殘
春　蠶　到　死　絲　方　盡
蠟　炬　成　灰　淚　始　乾
曉　鏡　但　愁　雲　鬢　改
夜　吟　應　覺　月　光　寒
蓬　山　此　去　無　多　路
青　鳥　殷　勤　為　探　看

Wu T'i
No Title

Hsiang chien shih nan pieh yi nan
Mutual see time hard part also hard
Tung feng wu li pai hua ts'an
East wind no power hundred flowers wither
Ch'un ts'an tao ssŭ ssŭ fang chin
Spring silkworm reach death silk only end
La chü ch'eng huei lei shih kan
Wax torch become ashes tears only dry
Hsiao ching tan ch'ou yun pin kai
Morning mirror but grieve cloudy hair change
Yeh yin ying chüeh yueh kuang han
Night recite should feel moon light cold
P'eng-shan tz'ŭ ch'ü wu to lu
P'eng Mountain here from not much way
Ch'ing-niao yin-ch'in wei t'an k'an
Blue Bird diligently for enquire see

Without Title

Hard it is for us to meet and hard to go away;
Powerless lingers the eastern wind as all the flowers decay.
The spring silkworm will only end his thread when death befalls;
The candle will drip with tears until it turns to ashes grey.
Facing the morning mirror, she fears her cloudy hair will fade;
Reading poems by night, she should be chilled by the moon's ray.
The fairy mountain P'eng lies at no great distance:
May a Blue Bird fly to her and my tender cares convey!

I shall have occasion to comment on this poem later (p. 137). For the time being, I shall merely point out that it follows the metrical rules described above, using one rime throughout and observing the tone pattern required.

Sometimes the middle couplets of a poem in Regulated Verse can be multiplied *ad infinitum* to form a kind of sequence known as P'ai Lü 排律 ('Regulated Verses in a Row'). On the other hand, four lines of Regulated Verse can form a poem in itself, called Chüeh Chü 絕句, which is sometimes translated as 'Stop-short Lines', but which I shall simply call a Quatrain, as the exact meaning of this term is not above dispute. Metrically, a Quatrain corresponds to half of an eight-line poem in Regulated Verse, but it must be emphasized that each Quatrain is a self-contained piece of writing and in no sense a truncated poem. The following is a seven-syllabic Quatrain by Wang Wei (699–759):

$$送\ 元\ 二\ 使\ 安\ 西$$
$$(\ 陽\ 關\ 曲\ )$$

渭	城	朝	雨	浥	輕	塵
客	舍	青	青	柳	色	新
勸	君	更	盡	一	杯	酒
西	出	陽	關	無	故	人

Sung Yuan Erh Shih Ah-hsi
Send-off Yuan Second Mission An-hsi

Wei ch'eng chao yü yi ch'ing ch'en (d'ien)
Wei town morning rain wet light dust
K'o shê ch'ing ch'ing liu sê hsin (sien)
Guest house green green willow colour fresh
Ch'üan chün keng chin yi pei chiu
Persuade you again finish a cup wine
Hsi ch'u Yang Kuan wu ku-jen (nzien)
West out Yang Gate no old-friend

Seeing Off Yuan Second on a Mission to An-hsi
(Also known as Song of the Yang Gate)

The light dust in the town of Wei is wet with morning rain;
Green, green, the willows by the guest house their yearly
    freshness regain.
Be sure to finish yet another cup of wine, my friend,
West of the Yang Gate no old acquaintance will you meet again!

Lyric Metres (Tz'ŭ 詞). The *tz'ŭ* is a genre of poetry which came into existence in T'ang times, and became an important vehicle for lyric poetry during the Five Dynasties (907–960) and the Sung dynasty (960–1278). The word *tz'ŭ* means no more than 'words (for singing)', and it is used to designate poetry written to existing music, in lines of unequal length, in contra-distinction to poetry in lines of equal length known as *shih*, such as the examples given above. To avoid using the rather awkward transliteration, I propose to translate *tz'ŭ* as Lyric Metres.

In writing poetry in Lyric Metres, the poet would choose a tune, or compose one himself, and then write words to it. Thus, instead of setting words to music, writers of Lyric Metres would 'fill in' (*t'ien*) the words to fit a given tune. A poem so written bears no title, but only the name of the tune, as if one should write new words to the tune of 'Green-sleeves' or 'Londonderry Air' and still call it by that name, though the new words usually bear no relation to the original name. Each tune dictated a separate tone pattern and rime scheme of its own, and a vast number of new metres were thus created. Most of the actual tunes used in Sung times have been lost, but the metres they gave rise to have survived. The *Ch'in Ting Tz'ŭ P'u*, a kind of handbook giving the tone patterns and rime schemes of the different metres, compiled by order of the Emperor Ch'ien Lung in the eighteenth century, gives the names of 826 tunes which gave rise to 2306 metres, including variant forms. Another work compiled by Wan Shu in the same period, the *Tz'ŭ Lü*, lists 875 tunes which gave rise to 1675 metres. This represents a tremendous development in Chinese versification, and though the music used is mostly lost, one can still 'fill in' the words demanded by these metres.

In a poem written in one of the Lyric Metres, the lines are often of unequal length, as I have observed, but the number of syllables in each line is fixed. It is therefore misleading to describe Lyric Metres as 'irregular' verse. Some liberty is allowed with regard to the tone pattern, but the rime scheme must be observed. In fact, Lyric Metres involve even stricter and much more complicated rules of versification than Regulated Verse, in spite of their appearance, especially in translation, of irregularity and freedom.

The following is a poem written to the tune *P'u-sa Man* ('Bod-
hisatva Barbarians') by Wei Chuang (836?–910):

人	人	盡	說	江	南	好
遊	人	只	合	江	南	老
	春	水	碧	於	天	
	畫	船	聽	雨	眠	
鑪	邊	人	似	月		
皓	腕	凝	霜	雪		
未	老	莫	還	鄉		
還	鄉	須	斷	腸		

Jen-jen chin shuo Chiang-nan hao
Man-man all say River-south good
Yu jen chih ho Chiang-nan lao
Wandering man only fit River-south old
Ch'un shuei pi yü t'ien
Spring water bluer than sky
Hua ch'uan t'ing yü mien
Painted boat hear rain sleep

Lu pien jen ssŭ yueh
Wine-jar side person like moon
Hao wan ning shuang hsüeh
Bright wrist frozen frost snow
Wei lao mo huan hsiang
Not-yet old do-not return home
Huan hsiang hsü tuan ch'ang
Return home must break bowels

Everyone is full of praise for the beauty of the South:
What can I do but end my days an exile in the South?
The spring river is bluer than the sky;
As it rains, in a painted barge I lie.

Bright as the moon is she who serves the wine;
Like frost or frozen snow her white wrists shine.
I'm not old yet: let me not depart!
For going home will surely break my heart!

I will discuss later the sentiments expressed in this poem
(p. 56). Meanwhile, I will just point out that the lines are grouped
in two stanzas, as shown above; the first two lines being seven-

syllabic, the rest being five-syllabic. The rime scheme is AABB CCDD. The tone pattern is as follows:

$$
\begin{array}{l}
- - / + + / - - + \text{A} \\
- - / + + / - - + \text{A} \\
\quad - + / + - - \text{B} \\
\quad + - / - + - \text{B} \\
\quad - - / - + + \text{C} \\
\quad + + / - - + \text{C} \\
\quad + + / + - - \text{D} \\
\quad - - / + + - \text{D}
\end{array}
$$

Dramatic Verse (*Ch'ü* 曲) and *Dramatic Lyrics* (*San-ch'ü* 散 曲). Dramatic poetry flourished during the Yuan or Mongol dynasty (1260–1341). As in the case of Lyric Metres, the dramatic poet would choose tunes from an existing repertoire and write words to them. These constitute the sung passages called *ch'ü*, in contrast to the spoken passages called *pai* 白 ('Plain Speech'). Dramatic Verse is metrically similar to Lyric Metres, but the tunes originally employed were from a different repertoire, which gave rise to another body of metres. Over five hundred such metres have survived, though most of the music that created them has not. In Dramatic Verse, the lines are of unequal length, and more liberty is allowed than in Lyric Metres regarding the number of syllables, for additional words may be inserted, known as *ch'en tzŭ* 襯 字 ('Padding Words'). Tone patterns and rime schemes, however, must be strictly observed. In view of the un-desirability of quoting dramatic passages out of context, I shall refrain from giving any example here.

Sometimes poets would write lyric pieces using metres normally employed in Dramatic Verse. Such compositions are called *san ch'ü* ('Loose Songs'), which I propose to translate as Dramatic Lyrics, even though they need not be dramatic in nature. The following is a brief Dramatic Lyric to the tune *T'ien Ching Sha* ('Sky Clear Sand') by Ma Chih-yuan (cir. 1270–1330):

枯　藤　老　樹　昏　鴉
小　橋　流　水　人　家
古　道　西　風　瘦　馬
　　夕　陽　西　下
斷　腸　人　在　天　涯

K'u t'eng lao shu hun ya
Withered vines old trees twilight crows
Hsiao ch'iao liu shuei jen chia
Little bridge flowing water people's house
Ku tao hsi feng shou ma
Ancient road west wind lean horse
    Hsi yang hsi hsia
    Evening sun west set
Tuan-ch'ang jen tsai t'ien ya
Broken-bowel man at heaven end

  Withered vines, aged trees, twilight crows.
Beneath the little bridge by the cottage the river flows.
On the ancient road and lean horse the west wind blows.
    The evening sun westward goes,
As a broken-hearted man stands at heaven's close.

One rime is used in this lyric, and the tone pattern is as follows:

$$- - / + + / - - \text{R}$$
$$+ - / - + / - - \text{R}$$
$$+ + / - - / + + \text{R}$$
$$\quad + - / - + \text{R}$$
$$+ - / - + / - - \text{R}$$

In addition to the above verse forms, there are others such as the *Sao* 騷 and the *Yueh-fu* 樂府. The *Sao* refers to imitations of the *Li Sao* ('Encountering Sorrow'),[1] the main work of Ch'ü Yuan (cir. 340–277 B.C.), who is the first great Chinese poet known by name and whose poems form the bulk of the anthology, *The Songs of Ch'u (Ch'u Tz'ŭ)*. The *Li Sao* is a long poem in six-syllabic couplets, the two lines of each couplet being connected by a meaningless syllable *hsi*.[2] The *Yueh-fu* refers to songs collected and edited by the Yueh-fu or 'Music Department', an office established by the Emperor Wu of Han (157–87 B.C.), as well as later folk songs of a similar nature. Metrically, the *Yueh-fu* songs are not radically different from the Ancient Verse, the main difference between the two being that the former were set to music and the latter was not. There is another kind of writing called the *Fu* 賦, which is not really a verse form

---

[1] The title has been interpreted in other ways, but this seems to me the most reasonable explanation.

[2] This is the modern pronunciation. It has been suggested that the original pronunciation was something like 'O'.

though it is often treated as if it were. The word *fu* means 'display', and is applied to compositions of a descriptive nature on given themes, in contrast to more spontaneous, lyrical pieces. It is impossible to define the *Fu* in purely formal terms, since not all pieces designated *Fu* have the same formal characteristics. The *Fu* of the Han dynasty is formally similar to the *Sao*, but some later writings also labelled *Fu* are in prose. It is therefore best not to take the *Fu* as a verse form but as a literary genre, and define it roughly as descriptions or expositions, usually lengthy and elaborate, in verse or in prose, on given subjects.

So far we have seen how the basic principles of versification are applied to various verse forms. We can now turn our attention to some specific auditory devices used in Chinese poetry.

Alliteration and Riming Compounds. Alliteration in Chinese poetry is usually confined to two syllables and known as *Shuang-sheng* 雙聲 ('Twin Sounds', the word 'sounds' here referring to the initial sounds of the syllables). Quite a few disyllabic words and compounds are alliterative, thus lending themselves easily to musical effect and finding favour with poets. They often occur in pairs, in antithetical couplets:

> P'iao-p'o *yu pei chiu*
> Ch'ih ch'u *tz'ŭ yi-t'ing*
> —Tu Fu

> (Wandering abroad, I still indulge in the cup;
> To and fro I pace in this post-pavilion.)

Here the alliterative *p'iao-p'o* ('wandering') and *ch'ih-ch'u* ('pace to and fro') stress the ideas of ceaseless wandering and bewildered hesitation respectively. Or take the following couplet:

> Jen-jan *hsing shuang huan*
> Huei-huan *chieh-hou ts'uei*
> —Po Chü-I

> (Alternately, stars and frost give way to each other;
> Round and round, the seasons hasten one another on.)

Obviously, the alliterative compounds *jen-jan* ('alternately') and *huei-huan* ('round and round') are used to stress the alternation of night and day and the revolution of the seasons.

Next to alliteration, riming compounds form another important device in Chinese prosody. The original term for this device is *Tieh-yun* 叠韻, which means literally 'double rime'. However, as it does not refer to end-rime, as in English, but to the use of compounds each consisting of two syllables that rime with one another, I have translated it as 'riming compounds', rather than as 'double rime'. Nor is this device the same as 'assonance', for it requires identical final consonants (if any) as well as similar vowels, while the latter only requires similar vowels, in two syllables. As in the case of alliteration, riming compounds usually occur in pairs in poetry:

> Wu-shu *hsing hsiang yin*
> Lian-shan *wang hu k'ai*
> —Tu Fu

> (The misty trees lead one on and on;
> The chained mountains suddenly open up.)

The riming compounds *wu-shu* ('misty trees') and *lian-shan* ('connected mountains') help to create an impression of endless stretches of trees and mountains. Similarly, in the next couplet, riming compounds are used to achieve a repetitive effect:

> *Chiang shan ch'eng* wan-chuan
> *Tung yü k'o* p'ai-huai
> —Tu Fu

> (Round the mountains and rivers the city-wall twists and turns;
> About the towers and halls I linger on and on.)

Here the riming compounds *wan-chuan* ('twist and turn') and *p'ai-huai* ('linger about') lend force to the description of the winding city-wall and the poet reluctant to leave.

Of course, riming compounds can sometimes be used simply for their pleasant sounds, without adding specifically to any descriptive effect. For example, in the following couplet:

> Fei-ts'uei *ming yi-hang*
> Ch'ing-t'ing *li tiao ssŭ*
> —Tu Fu

> (The kingfisher cries on the clothes-horse;
> The dragon-fly stands on the fishing line.)

one suspects that it was as much for the musical qualities of the names *fei-ts'uei* ('kingfisher') and *ch'ing-t'ing* ('dragon-fly') as for the visual beauty of these creatures that the poet chose to describe them in this poem.

In many cases, alliterative and riming compounds are used

together, in antithetical couplets. In the following couplet, the alliterative *yuan-yang* ('mandarin duck') is used to contrast with the riming *fei-ts'uei* ('kingfisher'):

> *Tien-wa* yuan-yang *ch'ê*
> *Kung-lien* fei-ts'uei *hsü*
> —Tu Fu

(On the palace tiles the mandarin ducks are cracked;
From the palace curtains the kingfishers are missing.)

In short, though alliteration and riming compounds are not essential features of Chinese prosody, they do occur quite often, and while it would be pedantic to claim that they invariably contribute to some particular effect, it remains true that they do enhance the general musical effect of poetry.

Reduplication. In Chinese, a monosyllabic word is sometimes reduplicated. Such words are called *Tieh-tzŭ* 叠 字 ('Reduplicated Words'). Three kinds may be distinguished. First, words repeated for emphasis, such as *chiao-chiao* 皎 皎 ('bright, bright'), *ch'i-ch'i* 凄 凄 ('chilly, chilly'), etc. Secondly, monosyllabic words reduplicated to form new compounds with independent meanings, such as *nien-nien* 年 年 ('year-year' = 'every year'), *yi-yi* 一 一 ('one-one' = 'one by one'), etc. Thirdly, words repeated in colloquial usage, without emphasis or change of meaning, such as *mei-mei* 妹 妹 for 'younger sister' instead of simply *mei*.

The use of reduplicated words in poetry has an effect akin to that of riming compounds. In fact, they can be regarded as an extreme form of riming compounds. Reduplications of the first kind occur naturally in poetry, as they do in prose, like:

> Ch'ing-ch'ing *ho-pan ts'ao*
> Yü-yü *yuan-chung liu*
> —The Nineteen Ancient Poems

(Green, green grows the grass by the river;
Thick, thick stand the willows in the garden.)

Such reduplications of course also occur in English, like 'long, long ago' or 'far, far away', but they are far more frequent in Chinese, to such an extent that some epithets are hardly ever used singly but always in reduplications.

Reduplicated words of the second kind, since they constitute compounds with independent meanings, are used as such in poetry, just as they are in prose. However, a poet can exploit the possibilities of verbal play that they afford. For instance, in describing a young bird that has lost its mother, Po Chü-I writes:

> Yeh-yeh yeh-pan *t'i*
> (Night after night, at midnight it cries.)

By putting the compound *yeh-yeh* ('night-night' = 'every night') immediately before *yeh-pan* ('night-half' = 'midnight'), the poet produces a daring stroke which at first startles the reader and then enables him to see the meaning. A similar play on words is used by Ou-yang Hsiu in a lyric describing a secluded boudoir:[1]

> *T'ing-yuan* shen-shen, shen *chi-hsü*?
> (Deep, deep lies the courtyard; how deep, one wonders?)

Awkward as this sounds in English, in the original it is an ingenious and delightful verbal play.

As for reduplications of the third kind, they are used in colloquial speech and not often encountered in poetry, except in some lyrics and dramatic verse. As they do not add anything to the poetic effect, no examples need by given.

Onomatopoeia. This occurs quite frequently in Chinese poetry, especially in early poetry. The very opening line of the first song in *The Book of Poetry* reads:

> Kuan kuan *chü-chiu*
> (*Kuan, kuan,* cry the ospreys.)

In another song in the same anthology, we read:

> Yao yao *ts'ao-ch'ung*
> (*Yao, yao,* cries the grasshopper.)

In later poetry, onomatopoeia is less often used, except in Yuan poetic drama. In the following lines from *Rain on the Wu-t'ung Trees* (*Wu-t'ung Yü*) by Pai P'u (1226–cir. 1313), onomatopoeia is used to reinforce similes describing the sound of rain falling on the trees:

> Ch'uang ch'uang *ssǔ pen-ch'üan jui-shou lin shuang-chao*;
> Shua shua *ssǔ shih-yeh ch'un-ts'an san man pao.*

(*Ch'uang, ch'uang*: like fabulous beasts sprouting water over twin ponds; *Shua, shua*: like spring silkworms feeding on leaves all over the frame.)

---

[1] This lyric also appears among the poems of Feng Yen-ssǔ, but the question of authorship does not concern us here.

To treat Chinese versification exhaustively is neither within the scope nor the intention of this book. However, some idea has been given above, I hope, of the auditory effects of Chinese verse. On the whole, Chinese verse has a stronger but perhaps less subtle music than English verse. The variation of tones creates a sing-song effect characteristic of Chinese, and in fact most Chinese readers *chant* rather than merely *read* verse aloud. At the same time, the relative paucity of vowels in Chinese and the lack of marked contrast between stressed and unstressed syllables render it more liable to monotony than English. Finally, the clear-cut quality of Chinese syllables, the absence of elision and liaison, and the fact that there are usually few syllables in each line, all tend to produce a *staccato* effect, unlike the more flowing, *legato* rhythms of English or French verse.

4

SOME GRAMMATICAL
ASPECTS OF THE
LANGUAGE OF POETRY

———————

G RAMMARIANS and poets are supposed to be traditional
enemies, yet in fact no enmity need exist between them. On
the contrary, grammarians can throw some light on the language
of poetry, without necessarily producing dry-as-dust analysis. In
this chapter, I propose to show how certain grammatical features
of the language of Chinese poetry add to its poetic effect, and how
the greater freedom from grammatical restrictions enjoyed by
Chinese bestows on it certain advantages over English as a
medium for poetry.

It has been alleged that Chinese has no grammar. To refute this,
one can do no better than quote the words of Sir Philip Sidney,
with which he answered the charge that English 'wanted
grammar':

> Nay truly, it has that prayse, that it wanteth not Grammar: for
> Grammar it might have, but it needes it not; being so easie of it selfe,
> and so voyd of those cumbersome differences of Cases, Genders,
> Moodes and Tenses, which I thinke was a peece of the Tower of
> Babilons curse, that a man should be put to school to learn his mother
> tongue.[1]

These words are even truer of Chinese than English, for after all
English is not entirely free from such cumbersome differences,

[1] *An Apologie for Poetrie.*

39

while Chinese, being a completely uninflected language, is not burdened with Cases, Genders, Moods, Tenses, etc. This is at once a source of strength and of weakness, for on the one hand it enables the writer to concentrate on essentials and be as concise as possible, while on the other hand it leads easily to ambiguity. In other words, where Chinese gains in conciseness, it loses in preciseness. As far as poetry is concerned, the gain is on the whole greater than the loss, for, as Aristotle observed, the poet is concerned with the universal rather than the particular, and the Chinese poet especially is often concerned with presenting the essence of a mood or a scene rather than with accidental details. For instance, in the lines

> *Yueh ch'u ching shan niao*
> Moon rise surprise mountain bird
> *Shih ming ch'un chien chung*
> Occasionally cry in spring valley
> —Wang Wei

it is of no consequence whether 'mountain', 'bird', and 'valley' are singular or plural: we can translate these lines as

> The moonrise surprises the mountain bird
> That cries now and again in the spring valley

or

> The moonrise surprises the mountain birds
> That cry now and again in the spring valley (or valleys).

As Chinese does not require any indication of 'number', the poet need not bother about such irrelevant details and can concentrate on his main task of presenting the spirit of a tranquil spring night among the mountains. Moreover, the absence of 'tense' in Chinese enables the poet to present the scene not from the point of view of any specific time but almost *sub specie aeternitatis*: we are not invited to watch a particular spring night scene viewed by a particular person at a certain point in time, but to feel the quintessence of 'spring-night-ness'.

This sense of timelessness and universality is further enhanced by the frequent omission of the subject of a verb in Chinese poetry. Take for example the following Quatrain by Wang Wei:

> *K'ung shan pu chien jen*
> Empty mountain not see people
> *Tan wen jen yü hsiang*
> Only hear people talk sound

> *Fan ying ju shen lin*
> Reflected light enter deep forest
> *Fu chao ch'ing t'ai shang*
> Again shine green moss upon

The poet simply says 'not see people', not 'I do not see anyone' or even 'One does not see anyone'; consequently no awkward questions such as 'If no one is here, who is hearing the voices?' or 'If you are here, how can the mountains be said to be empty?' will occur to the reader. Instead, he is made to feel the presence of Nature as a whole, in which the mountains, the human voices, the sunlight, the mosses, are all equals. To preserve this sense of impersonality in English, one has to resort to the 'passive voice':

> On the empty mountains no one can be seen,
> But human voices are heard to resound.
> The reflected sunlight pierces the deep forest
> And falls again upon the mossy ground.

Such omissions of the subject allows the poet not to intrude his own personality upon the scene, for the missing subject can be readily identified with anyone, whether the reader or some imaginary person. Consequently, Chinese poetry often has an impersonal and universal quality, compared with which much Western poetry appears egocentric and earth-bound. Where Wordsworth wrote '*I* wander*ed* lonely as *a* cloud', a Chinese poet would probably have written simply 'Wander as cloud'. The former records a personal experience bound in space and time; the latter presents a state of being with universal applications.

Sometimes even verbs are omitted in Chinese poetry, and lines can consist of a series of nouns shed of all the connecting links such as conjunctions, verbs, and particles required by prose grammar. For instance, in the short Dramatic Lyric I quoted once before (p. 33), the first three lines consist of nothing but nouns with adjectives:

> Withered vines, old trees, twilight crows,
> Little bridge, flowing water, people's house,
> Ancient road, west wind, lean horse.

In my translation, partly for the sake of rime and partly to make it read more smoothly, I added a few verbs and prepositions:

> Withered vines, aged trees, twilight crows.
> Beneath the little bridge by the cottage the river flows.
> On the ancient road and lean horse the west wind blows.

Here, the poet unfolds a scene like a scroll of Chinese painting, and our attention moves from one object to the next, yet the absence of verbs creates a sense of stillness in movement, as if these objects had been arrested in time and frozen in an eternal pose, like those figures on the Grecian urn immortalized by Keats.

The omission of verbs and particles is but one way in which the syntax of Chinese poetry, especially that of Regulated Verse, differs from that of prose. For example, whereas in prose the subject normally precedes the verb, in poetry the two can be inverted:

> *Chu hsüan kwei huan nü*
> Bamboo make-noise, return washer-women
> *Lien tung hsia yü chou*
> Lotus move, down-come fishing boats
> —Wang Wei

Here the subjects 'washer-women' and 'fishing boats' are placed after the verbs, and no conjunction is used to join the two clauses in each line. In prose, one would have to write something like

> *Chu hsüan erh huan nü kwei*
> Bamboo make-noise and washer-women return
> *Lien tung erh yü chou hsia*
> Lotus move and fishing boats come-down

In English translation, too, one could hardly dispense with conjunctions:

> Bamboos rustle as the washer-women return;
> Lotuses move, and down come the fishing boats.

Such inversions in Chinese represent a further departure from prose syntax than do similar inversions in English, for in English prose one does place the verb before the subject sometimes, while in Chinese one seldom does.

Furthermore, inversions in poetry not only make for greater compression and economy of words but help to achieve variation in rhythm within the strait-jacket of metrical rules. By changing the syntax, the poet can modify the caesura and thus break away from the monotony that would otherwise result from a strict observance of the rules of versification. In describing the rules of Regulated Verse, I marked the caesura after the second syllable in a five-syllabic line (p. 26). This is the basic rhythm, variations from which can be achieved by shifting the caesura or adding a minor pause as required by the syntax. For example, in the couplet

> *Ming-yueh sung-chien chao*
> Bright moon pines among shine
> *Ch'ing-ch'üan shih-shang liu*
> Clear fountain rocks upon flow
> —Wang Wei

> (The bright moon shines among the pines;
> The clear fountain flows upon the rocks)

the basic rhythm is:

$$- + / - - +$$
$$- - / + + -$$

but in addition, a slight pause is required after the fourth syllable as well, making the rhythm

$$- + / - - / +$$
$$- - / + + / -$$

In the next couplet, an additional pause is required after the third syllable:

> *Ch'an-sheng chi ku-ssŭ*
> Cicada sound gather ancient temple
> *Niao-ying tu han-t'ang*
> Bird shadow cross cold pond
> —Tu Fu

> (Cicadas' cries gather in the ancient temple;
> A bird's shadow crosses the cold pond.)

Here the rhythm becomes:

$$- - / - / + +$$
$$+ + / + / - -$$

Thus, within the framework of orthodox versification, a poet can achieve subtle variations of rhythm by modifying the mechanical rhythm of the metre with syntactical changes. Just as Shakespeare produced great rhythmic variety without discarding the basic pattern of blank verse, so did Chinese poets produce similar effects without doing away with the rules of Regulated Verse.[1]

---

[1] Readers who know Chinese may consult Wang Li's *Han-yü Shih-lü Hsüeh*, pp. 230–3, for a list of variations.

The above observations apply also to Lyric Metres. Take the following lyric written to the tune *Keng Lou Tz'ŭ* ('Song of the Water-clock at Night') by Wen T'ing-yun (812?–870?):

> *Liu-ssŭ ch'ang*
> Willow silk long
> *Ch'un-yü hsi*
> Spring rain fine
> *Hua-wai lou-sheng t'iao-ti*
> Flower-beyond clock-sound long
> *Ching sai-yen*
> Surprise frontier-geese
> *Ch'i ch'eng-wu*
> Arouse city-wall-crows
> *Hua-p'ing chin chê-ku*
> Painted-screen golden partridges
>
> *Hsiang-wu po*
> Fragrant mist thin
> *T'ou lien-mo*
> Penetrate curtain
> *Ch'ou-ch'ang Hsieh-chia ch'ih ko*
> Sorrowful Hsieh-family pond pavilion
> *Hung-chu pei*
> Red candle back
> *Hsiu-lien ch'uei*
> Embroidered curtain droop
> *Meng ch'ang chün pu chih*
> Dream long you not know

The willow twigs are long,
The spring rain is drizzling,
While endless runs the water-clock beyond the flowers.
Rousing the crows on the citadel,
The wild geese on the frontier,
And the golden partridges on the painted screen.

A light fragrant mist
Drifts in through the curtain:
The ponds and pavilions of the Hsiehs are full of sorrow.
Sheltered from the candle,
Behind the embroidered curtain,
Long I dream, but you are unaware!

In this lyric, metrical rules demand that lines 1 and 2 and lines 4 and 5 in the first stanza should respectively observe the following tone patterns:

$$+ - -$$
$$- + + \text{ (lines 1 and 2)}$$
$$- + +$$
$$+ - - \text{ (lines 4 and 5)}$$

This our poet has done. In addition, he has worked out a different pause in each case: lines 1 and 2 have a pause after the second syllable:

> *Liu-ssŭ* | *ch'ang*
> Willow-silk | long
> *Ch'un-yü* | *hsi*
> Spring-rain | fine

while lines 4 and 5 have a pause after the first syllable:

> *Ching* | *sai-yen*
> Surprise | frontier-geese
> *Ch'i* | *ch'eng-wu*
> Arouse | city-wall-crows

Thus, not only do we get the contrast of tones between

$$+ - -$$
$$- + +$$

and

$$- + +$$
$$+ - -$$

but also a variation in the position of the caesura:

$$+ - / -$$
$$- + / +$$

in contrast to

$$- / + +$$
$$+ / - -$$

One could give endless examples, but I think enough has been said to show that syntactical changes can help to achieve variations in rhythm.

Another grammatical feature of the language of poetry, one that is closely connected with its syntax, is the fluidity of 'parts of speech'. In Chinese prose, words already enjoy a high degree of freedom in this respect, and the same word can be used as noun, verb, adjective, etc., according to the context. This freedom is increased in poetry. For instance, in a poem describing the capital Ch'ang-an after it had fallen to the rebels, Tu Fu wrote:

> *Kuo p'o shan ho tsai*
> Country broken, mountains rivers exist
> *Ch'eng ch'un ts'ao mu shen*
> City spring, grass trees deep

Here, *ch'un* ('spring') is used as adjective to modify 'city', in contrast to the 'broken' of the preceding line. The gain in compactness and vividness is obvious: it is as if one were to write 'city spring-ed' instead of 'city in spring' or 'spring in the city'.

Moreover, since adjectives can be used verbally in Chinese, in many cases where one would have to use the copula in English, there is no need for anything corresponding to it in Chinese. For instance, in Chinese one habitually says the equivalent of 'Flowers red' instead of that of 'Flowers *are* red'. The former is at once more concise and more forceful than the latter.

A further advantage of using the same word as different parts of speech is that one can keep exactly the same implications and associations, instead of searching for another word with similar ones. For example, the word *shih* ('master') carries with it all the traditional implications of reverence, obedience, and affection, and when it is used as a verb, apart from meaning 'to learn from', it carries the same implications. To translate it into English, one would have to paraphrase and say 'to serve as master' or 'to follow as master', but even so one could hardly keep all the implications of the word. Also, by using nouns verbally, one can render the description more concrete. This of course is also true of English: to 'elbow' is more concrete than to 'nudge', and to 'finger' is more vivid than to 'touch'. Only, one can do this much more frequently in Chinese.

To sum up: Chinese grammar is fluid, not architectural. Whereas in a highly inflected language such as Latin, words are solid bricks with which to build complicated edifices of periods and paragraphs, in Chinese they are chemical elements which form new compounds with great ease. A Chinese word cannot be pinned down to a 'part of speech', 'gender', 'case', etc., but is a mobile unit which acts on, and reacts with, other units in a constant flux. This enables Chinese poets to write with the greatest possible conciseness, and at the same time achieve an impersonal and universal quality by dispensing with all accidental trappings. Thus, into a sequence of merely some twenty or thirty syllables can be compressed the essence of a scene, a mood, a whole experience; and it is not too much to claim that in a Chinese Quatrain or short lyric one does 'see a world in a grain of sand'.

5

SOME CHINESE CONCEPTS
AND WAYS OF
THINKING AND FEELING

I N the preceding chapters we have considered various aspects of
the Chinese language itself—visual, semantic, auditory, and
grammatical—in so far as they affect the nature of Chinese poetry.
Yet no full understanding of a language, let alone the poetry
written in it, is possible without some knowledge of its under-
lying concepts and ways of thinking and feeling, which can be
revealed in the commonest expressions in the language. For in-
stance, in Chinese, instead of saying 'length', 'height', 'width',
etc., one says 'long-short-ness', 'high-low-ness', 'wide-narrow-
ness', etc., which show a dualistic world-concept and a relativistic
way of thinking. Furthermore, different concepts and ways of
thinking and feeling, in their turn, cannot be fully understood
without reference to social and cultural environments. It is of
course impossible to enquire deeply into all these questions here;
the most I can hope to do in this chapter is to discuss a few
typically Chinese concepts and ways of thinking and feeling which
often form the actual themes or underlying frameworks of Chinese
poetry and which might be misunderstood by Western readers,
and I shall only touch upon social and cultural conditions when the
need arises. As for ideas and feelings which are universal and
easily understood, such as the sorrow of parting and the horror
of war, they need not be discussed.

NATURE

In Chinese poetry, as in the poetry in other languages, there abound innumerable pieces describing the beauties of Nature and expressing joy over them. Such straightforward poems need no comment. However, in the works of some Chinese poets, such as T'ao Ch'ien (372-427) and Wang Wei (701-761), Nature assumes a deeper significance, a significance quite different from that perceived by English 'Nature poets', notably Wordsworth.

In the first place, Nature to these Chinese poets is not a physical manifestation of its Creator, as it is to Wordsworth, but something that is what it is by virtue of itself. The Chinese term for 'Nature' is *tzŭ-jan*, or 'Self-thus', and the Chinese mind seems content to accept Nature as a fact, without searching for a *primum mobile*. This concept of Nature somewhat resembles Thomas Hardy's 'Immanent Will', but without its rather sombre and gloomy associations.

From this it follows that Nature is neither benignant nor hostile to Man. Hence, Man is not conceived of as for ever struggling against Nature but forming part of it. There are no Icaruses and Fausts in Chinese poetry; instead, Man is advised to submerge his being in the infinite flux of things and to allow his own life and death to become part of the eternal cycle of birth, growth, decline, death, and re-birth that goes on in Nature. This is clearly expressed by T'ao Ch'ien in a poem entitled 'Form, Shadow, and Spirit', in which Form represents the *popular* Taoist wish for the elixir of life and physical immortality, Shadow expounds the Confucian ideal of achieving immortality through great deeds and permanent fame, while Spirit expresses the poet's own view:

> Let yourself drift on the stream of Change,
> Without joy and without fear.
> When the end is due, let it come;
> No need to worry any more then.

Furthermore, in the works of such poets, Nature is not viewed from a personal angle at a particular time, but as it always is. The presence of the poet is withdrawn or unobtrusively submerged in the total picture. I have already demonstrated this point on p. 41, and the lines from Wang Wei quoted there may bear it out.

But these poets are exceptional even among the Chinese, not all of whom are able to attain to this self-less state of contemplation. Instead, they sigh over the brevity of human life as contrasted with the abiding features of Nature. Indeed, it is this contrast between the mutability and transiency of human life on the one hand and the permanence and eternal renewal of the life of Nature on the other that gives much Chinese poetry a special poignancy and endows it with a tragic sense, whereas in Western poetry, such as in Greek tragedy and Romantic poetry, it is often the conflict between Man and Nature and the frustration of Man's efforts to overcome the limitations that Nature has set him that gives rise to tragedy. This leads us to our next point for consideration: sense of time in Chinese poetry.

TIME

Most Chinese poetry displays a keen awareness of time, and expresses regret over its irretrievable passing. Of course, Western poets are sensitive to time too, but few of them seem to be as obsessed by it as Chinese poets generally are. Moreover, a Chinese poem often gives more clear and precise indications of the season and the time of day than a Western poem normally does. There are hundreds of Chinese poems lamenting the fading away of spring, grieving over the coming of autumn, or dreading the approach of old age. The falling of spring petals, the withering of autumn leaves, the glimmering of the last rays of the setting sun—all these invariably remind the sensitive Chinese poet of 'Time's winged chariot' and arouse apprehensions of the passing away of his own youth and the onset of old age and death. A naïve expression of such feelings is the famous *Song of the Autumn Wind* by the Emperor Wu of Han (157–87 B.C.):

The autumn wind rises, scattering white clouds in the sky;
The grass and trees turn yellow and shed their leaves, the wild geese
  southward fly.
But the orchids retain their beauty, the chrysanthemums their fragrance yet:
How they remind me of the lovely lady whom I cannot forget!
Upon the Fen River our ships their sails unfold—
Our ships that float mid-stream, rousing waves white and bold.
To the sound of flutes and drums the boatmen sing as the oars they
  hold.
Having reached the summit of joy, I feel sorrows untold:
How long will youth endure, and how could one help growing old?

A more sophisticated expression of regret over the pasage of time is the following lyric written to the tune *Huan Hsi Sha* ('Washing Brook Sand') by the poetess Li Ch'ing-chao (1081?–cir. 1150):[1]

All over the roof hangs the blue sunny sky;
Before the door, the fragrant herbs adjoining the horizon lie.
O do not ascend to the top of the staircase high!

The new shoots have grown into bamboos beneath the steps;
The fallen flowers have all gone into the swallows' nests near by.
—How can one bear to hear beyond the woods the cuckoo's cry?

Here, both the emotions and the way they are expressed are subtle. In the first stanza, the luxuriant growth of the fragrant herbs that extend as far as the horizon gives the first hint at the passing away of spring. At the same time, it also suggests longing for an absent lover, through its contextual association with two lines from the *Songs of Ch'u*: 'The young nobleman is wandering abroad and will not return; the fragrant herbs are again flourishing.' That is why in the next line the poetess warns herself not to ascend the staircase to look afar, for even if she could see as far as the horizon, all she would find would be the fragrant herbs but no traces of the young man. In the second stanza, the suggestion that spring is passing away is followed up by the maturity of the bamboo shoots, the use of the fallen flowers by the swallows to fortify their nests, and the cry of the cuckoo. All these help to deepen the note of wistfulness, already present in the first stanza, by suggesting that the youth and beauty of the poetess would also fade away like spring. Furthermore, the cuckoo is associated with unhappy love because of the legend that an ancient emperor of Shu, Emperor Wang, fell in love with the wife of one of his ministers and was metamorphosed into this bird after his death. Finally, the cry of the cuckoo is supposed to sound like the words 'Pu ju kuei' ('Better return home'), and thus becomes here a plea on behalf of the poetess to the absent wanderer.

Poems like the above two might seem to Western readers to express little more than sentimental self-pity, but they become more understandable, if not justified, when one remembers that most Chinese intellectuals feel no assurance of immortality. The

[1] This poem has also been attributed to Chou Pang-yen, but I am inclined to assign it to the poetess Li Ch'ing-chao, as the sentiments and sensibility shown in the poem seem particularly feminine.

true Taoists seek a return to the infinite flux of the life of Nature rather than personal survival; the Buddhists aim at a cessation of all consciousness; the Confucians have little to say about life after death. (The Confucian insistence on ancestral worship does not necessarily imply a belief in life after death, for this is meant as an outward sign of remembrance and is often practised as a moral obligation rather than as religious observance.) Poets who were unable to find solace in Taoism or Buddhism and to resign themselves calmly to the fate of all common mortals can but lament the passing of time and dread the approach of the inevitable end. Yet, paradoxically enough, just because this life is finite and brief, it seems all the more precious and worth living. While bemoaning the transiency of life, Chinese poets are at the same time determined to make the best of it while it lasts. This attitude may partly account for the extraordinary sensibility to, and minute observation of, Nature, such as shown in the last quoted poem.

History

Not only do we find in Chinese poetry a keen awareness of personal existence in time, but also a strong sense of history; after all, what is history if not the record of a nation's collective consciousness of its own temporal existence? On the whole, Chinese poets feel towards history much in the same way as they do towards personal life: they contrast the rise and fall of dynasties with the apparently permanent features of Nature; they sigh over the futility of heroic deeds and princely endeavours; they shed tears over battles fought long ago or beauties long dead, 'les neiges d'antan'. Poems expressing such sentiments are usually labelled 'poems recalling antiquity' (*huai ku shih* 懷古詩). They differ from the so-called 'poems on history' (*yung shih shih* 詠史詩), which generally point a moral or use some historical event as an excuse for comment on contemporary political affairs. The following Quatrain by Li Po is a typical 'poem recalling antiquity':

Viewing an Ancient Site in Yueh

After conquering Wu, the King of Yueh returned in triumph:
All his chivalrous warriors were clad in silk on coming home;
The Court ladies, like blossoms, filled the palace in spring,
Where now only a few partridges are flying about.

One could give many more examples, but perhaps one is enough, as such poems tend to express the same kind of feeling with the same kind of technique: stressing the vanity of human endeavours by contrasting the glories of the past with the ruins of to-day. This kind of poetry is of course by no means unique; one comes across similar examples in Western poetry. But where a Western poet might moralize about the frailty of human achievements in contrast to the eternal power of God, a Chinese poet is usually content to lament the former and leave it at that. Some agnostic European poets, however, come very close to the Chinese attitude. Shelley's *Ozymandias*, for instance, would pass admirably for a 'poem recalling antiquity'; so would Housman's *Wenlock Edge* with its typical ending:

> To-day the Roman and his trouble
> Are ashes under Uricon.

LEISURE

The word *hsien* 閒, here tentatively rendered as 'leisure', is sometimes also translated as 'idleness'. However, when used in poetry, it carries no derogatory implications, and can mean more than just being unoccupied, but a state of mind free from worldly cares and desires and at peace with itself and with Nature. Perhaps 'being in peace' is a better translation. It is one of the key words in the poetry of Wang Wei, as the following couplets from some of his poems will help to show:

> In silence heaven and earth are growing dusk;
> My mind, with the broad stream, lies *in peace*.

> My mind, ever *peaceful*, is made more so
> By the clear stream that lies so calm.

> The clear stream washes the tall thicket;
> Carriages and horses pass by *in peace*.

> Man *in peace*, cassia flowers fall;
> Night quiet, spring hill is empty.

From these lines one can perceive how the poet has emptied his mind of worries and desires and identified it with the objects around him: everything, from the great river to the passing traffic and the falling flowers, seems as calm and peaceful as his own mind. There is no sense of regret at the poet's idleness, nor is there even any suggestion of sadness, as in many other Chinese poems, that the river is flowing away and never coming back and that the flowers are falling. Wang Wei has, in fact, raised *hsien* to the level of philosophic and aesthetic contemplation, a state of mind even higher and more positive than the kind of indolence Keats celebrated, with its rejection of Love, Ambition, and Poesy.

However, in the works of some other Chinese poets, *hsien* has no such philosophic import. Rather, it signifies a nonchalant, list-less, and wistful state of mind that resembles 'ennui'. For instance, in the following lyric to the tune *Tieh Lüan Hua* by Feng Yen-ssŭ, 'idle feeling' (*hsien ch'ing*) has nothing to do with philosophic contemplation:

> Who says that this idle feeling has long been left aside?
> Whenever spring comes, my melancholy returns as before.
> Every day, before the flowers, I'm ill with too much drinking,
> Yet dare I refuse to let my image in the mirror grow thin?
>
> O you green grass by the river and willows on the dam,
> Pray tell me: why does new sorrow arise with each year?
> Alone on a little bridge I stand, my sleeves filled with wind;
> The new moon rises above the woods and everyone else is gone.

Some commentators would have us believe that this poem is allegorical, that the poet, who was Prime Minister of the Kingdom of Southern T'ang, was worried about his country. This seems to me too far-fetched. Indeed, Chinese critics are only too apt to impose an allegorical interpretation on any poem. Let us take the poem simply as a lyric: the poet is troubled with a nameless, groundless, 'idle feeling'—a feeling of ennui, of *langueur*, of a 'deuil sans raison'. To drown it, he is drinking himself to death (or so he thinks). Yet he takes a masochistic pleasure in pining away like this (and who can blame him for enjoying such a pleasant way of pining away?) and he even considers it a moral obligation to do so ('dare I refuse?'). This sophisticated emotional attitude, so reminiscent of late nineteenth-century European *decadence*, is re-vealed in a language no less sophisticated. Notice, among other things, how the poet speaks of letting his image in the mirror grow thin, instead of himself. This kind of poetry seeks to cap-ture subtle and elusive moods and to explore complex and indefinable emotions which could only exist in a highly cultured, aristocratic, and (yes!) *leisured milieu*. Here, *hsien* has all the social and cultural implications of 'leisure' as in 'a lady of leisure'. At the same time, it is tinged with gentle melancholy, which makes it different from the frivolity of 'idle singers of an empty day'.

NOSTALGIA

No one who has read any amount of Chinese poetry, even in translation, can fail to notice the abundance of poems on nostalgia. Chinese poets seem to be perpetually bewailing their exile and longing to return home. This again may seem sentimental to Western readers, but one should remember the vastness of China, the difficulties of communication that existed, the sharp contrast between the highly cultured life in the main cities and the harsh conditions in the remoter regions of the country, and the importance of the family in traditional Chinese society with the consequent deep attachment to the ancestral home. Moreover, being an agricultural people and a nation of landlubbers, the Chinese as a whole are noticeably lacking in *Wanderlust*. It is not surprising, therefore, that nostalgia should have become a constant, and hence conventional, theme in Chinese poetry. Once it became a conventional theme, it was only natural that some poets and poetasters should have written nostalgic verse with little justification, when they were living only a hundred miles or so from home and under extremely comfortable circumstances. However, the existence of conventionally nostalgic verse in Chinese does not invalidate poems that express homesickness genuinely felt.

It would be easy to give many examples of poems on this theme. Numerous lines come readily to mind, such as Li Po's well-known

> Raising my head, I look at the bright moon;
> Bending my head, I think of my old home.

To make it more interesting, I will give as examples not straightforward expressions of homesickness, but one poem which expresses such emotion indirectly, and another which contrasts nostalgia with the pleasures of the moment.

The first poem is written to the tune *Keng Lou Tzŭ*, by Wen

T'ing-yun, another poem by whom in the same metre has been given on p. 44:

> The tower stands by the river,
> The moon shines on the sea,
> Upon the city-wall a horn is sobbing soft.
> The willows wave on the dam,
> The islands are dim with mist,
> Two lines of travelling wild geese fly apart.
>
> By the Hsi-ling road
> Passes the homeward sail:
> It is the time when flowers and herbs begin to fade.
> The silver candle exhausted,
> The Jade Rope hanging low,
> From the village comes the cock's crow.

In this lyric the feeling of nostalgia is brought out by means of imagery and associations rather than direct statement. In the first stanza, the sad blowing of the horn in line 3 suggests a solitary guard at some frontier city; the willows in line 4, as I have remarked before (p. 11), are associated with parting; the wild geese in line 6 are often used as a symbol of distant journey and exile. In the second stanza, the ship carrying someone else home contrasts with the poet's own homelessness; the fading of the flowers and herbs adds to the mood of sadness by indicating the passing away of spring; and in the last three lines the burnt-out candle, the low hanging stars (the Jade Rope being the name of a constellation), and the cock's crow at dawn all suggest a sleepless night.

The second example is the lyric to the tune *P'u-sa Man* by Wei Chuang, which I have given on p. 31. Here I shall only repeat the verse translation:

> Everyone is full of praise for the beauty of the South;
> What can I do but end my days an exile in the South?
> The spring river is bluer than the sky;
> As it rains, in a painted barge I lie.
>
> Bright as the moon is she who serves the wine;
> Like frost or frozen snow her white wrists shine.
> I'm not old yet: let me not depart!
> For going home will surely break my heart!

The poet, it should be explained, had escaped from his native district near the capital Ch'ang-an in North China during the rebellion of Huang Ch'ao and was now living in the South, i.e. south of the Yangtze River, a part of the country renowned for its natural beauty and its lovely maidens. While longing to go home, the poet was at the same time enchanted by the scenery and the girl 'bright as the moon' before him. His conflicting emotions thus create a tension which underlies the otherwise simple and straightforward poem.

LOVE

Some Western translators, it seems to me, have over-emphasized the importance of friendship between men in Chinese poetry and correspondingly underestimated that of love between man and woman. True, there are many Chinese poems by men professing affection for other men in terms which would bring serious embarrassment if not public prosecution to an English poet; true also that in old China, where marriages were arranged by the parents, a man's needs for sympathy, understanding, and affection often found their answer in another man; nevertheless, many men did feel true love for women, if not always for their wives, and there *is* a great deal of love poetry in Chinese. *The Book of Poetry* is full of outspoken love songs; so are anthologies of folk songs of the Han and the Six Dynasties. Nor did love poetry diminish in later periods: it abounds in the works of such T'ang and Sung poets as Li Shang-yin, Wen T'ing-yun, Liu Yung, Huang T'ing-chien, and a host of others, not to mention the Yuan and Ming dramatic poets. In short, love is a theme as inevitable in Chinese poetry as it is in Western poetry, but where the Chinese conception of love seems to differ from the European one (or at least the Romantic European one) is that the former does not exalt love as something absolute that frees the person in love from all moral responsibilities. Nor is it usually regarded as an outward sign of spiritual union, as it is in some of the Metaphysical Poets. The Chinese attitude towards love is sensible and realistic: love is given its proper place in life as an essential and valuable experience but not elevated above everything else. Chinese poetry sings of love in its manifold phases: the thrill of the first encounter, the yearning for the loved one, the torment of uncertainty, the ecstasy of fulfilment, the agony of separation, the humiliation and bitterness of being deserted, the final despair of bereavement. Love in Chinese poetry can be serious or light-hearted, tender or passionate, even frankly erotic at times, but seldom, if ever, Platonic. Most aspects of love found their expression in that great poetic drama *Romance of the Western Chamber* (*Hsi Hsiang Chi*), but since no snippets can do it justice, I shall refrain from quoting from this masterpiece but content myself with giving two more lyrics by Wen T'ing-yun to the tune *Keng Lou Tzŭ*.

> A golden pin on her hair,
> Pink and white her face,
> She came to meet me for a moment among the flowers.
> 'You understand my feelings—'
> 'I'm grateful for your pity—'
> Heaven alone can witness this love of ours!

> The incense burnt to ashes,
> The candle dissolved in tears:
> These are what our hearts are like, yours and mine!
> My pillow lying smooth,
> My silk coverlet cold,
> I wake up when the night is almost gone.

> •   •   •   •

> An incense-burner of jade,
> A red candle in tears:
> Why do they reflect autumn thoughts in the painted room?
> Her eyebrows losing their colour,
> Her cloudy hair dishevelled,
> Her pillow and quilt grow cold in the lengthy night.

> Upon the *wu-t'ung* trees
> The midnight rain is beating,
> Indifferent to the bitter sorrow of parted lovers.
> Leaf after leaf,
> Drop after drop—
> They fall on the empty steps till break of day.

RAPTURE WITH WINE

Again, as every reader of Chinese poetry must be aware, there are constant references in it to drinking and becoming *tsuei*, which is usually translated as 'drunk', though actually it carries rather different implications and associations. The word does not imply gross sensual enjoyment, nor does it suggest hilarity and conviviality, as do many European drinking songs. The character *tsuei* 醉 consists of a pictogram for a wine-jar 酉 and a phonetic *tsu* 卒, which by itself means 'finish' or 'reach the limit'. According to the *Shuo Wen*, a philological work of about A.D. 100 and the cornerstone of Chinese etymology, the phonetic here is also significant, and the whole composite character is explained as meaning 'everyone reaching the limit of his capacity without offending propriety'. Even if we do not accept this explanation, it still remains true that in poetry *tsuei* does not mean quite the same thing as 'drunk', 'intoxicated', or 'inebriated', but rather means being mentally carried away from one's normal preoccupations. Of course these English words can also be used metaphorically: one can be 'drunk with success' or 'intoxicated with beauty', but when used by themselves they do not have the same feeling as *tsuei*. I therefore prefer not to use any of these words but to translate *tsuei* as 'rapt with wine'.

In saying the above I am not suggesting that the Chinese never get drunk. Whether Chinese people get drunk or not in real life is one thing; what the Chinese poets mean when they write that they are *tsuei* is quite another. Being *tsuei* in Chinese poetry is largely a matter of convention, and it would be as wise to take literally a Chinese poet's professed 'drunkenness' as to accept at their face value an Elizabethan sonneteer's complaints of his mistress's cruelty. This convention goes back at least as far as *The Fisherman*, a piece in the anthology *The Songs of Ch'u*, formerly attributed to Ch'ü Yuan but probably a forgery of the first century B.C. In this, the poet complains, 'The whole world is "drunk", but I alone am sober'. Later poets like Liu Ling inverted the positions of the poet and of the world, and sought *tsuei* as a symbol of escape from the miseries of the world and from one's personal emotions. In one of his famous poems on drinking, T'ao Ch'ien expresses very clearly this escapist attitude:

> Two travellers there are, often seen together,
> Yet they have widely different tastes.
> One, a scholar, is often rapt with wine,
> The other, a plain man, sober all the year.
> The rapt and the sober laugh at each other,
> And neither would listen to what the other says.
> How foolish is he so rigid and proper!
> The haughty one is the wiser of the two.
> Take my advice, you that are flushed with wine,
> When the sun sets, light your candles up!

In a similar vein, Li Po writes:

> Living in this world is a great dream,
> Why exert oneself to shorten one's life?
> That is why I'm rapt with wine all day
> And lie happily by the front pillars of the hall.
> Waking up, I look at the courtyard:
> A single bird is singing among the flowers.
> Pray tell me, bird, what day is this?
> —The oriole keeps singing in the spring breeze.
> Moved by this scene, I wish to sigh,
> But pour out another cup of wine instead.
> I sing aloud to wait for the bright moon;
> My song over, all my feelings are gone.

Are these the boisterous songs of habitual drunkards?

PART II

Some Traditional Chinese Views
on Poetry

INTRODUCTORY

To write a complete history of the criticism of Chinese poetry would require a volume probably several times the size of the present one and would involve long and intricate discussions on abstruse concepts and technical details. Such, therefore, is not my purpose in this part of the book. What I intend to do is to present a few views on poetry, which seem to me to be the most important ones. I shall pay special attention to some critics of later periods, who often summed up the opinions of their predecessors and in whose writings certain trends of thought with long traditions reached their culminations, rather than trace in detail the development of each trend through successive ages.

My task is made difficult by the fact that Chinese critics of the past seldom expounded their theories of poetry in a very systematic manner, but were content to let their views be scattered among 'Poetry Talks' (*Shih-hua*), notes, letters, reported conversations, and prefaces to anthologies and to their own or other people's works. Some of these scattered writings have been collected by modern Chinese literary historians, who have, however, not greatly elucidated the ideas contained in them. Moreover, most of the critics did not bother to define their terms clearly, not even the key words of their theories. And when one tries to discuss these terms in a language other than Chinese, the problem of how to translate them appears at first sight well-nigh insoluble, for to translate is to interpret and define. I shall make no direct effort to define all such terms; instead, I shall tackle the problem from another angle, by asking two questions about poetry and trying to find out from the writings of various critics how they would have answered. The first question is what poetry is, or should be; and the second, how one should write poetry, or, more specifically, what matters most in the writing of poetry, whether it is inspiration, or emotion, or technique, or anything else. In order not to confuse and bore the reader, I shall not enumerate all my sources and quote endless passages, but synthesize the results of my studies and give a somewhat more coherent account of these critics' views than can be found in their own writings. In so doing I shall endeavour to be as impartial as possible, and if I should still misrepresent or over-simplify any of their ideas, I could but beg the forgiveness of their departed souls and the forbearance of the reader!

THE DIDACTIC VIEW:
POETRY AS MORAL
INSTRUCTION AND
SOCIAL COMMENT

———

To the question what poetry is, most orthodox Confucians would reply: it is primarily a kind of moral instruction. And since government by moral influence is a Confucian political ideal, the function of poetry also includes comment on social and political affairs. Those who hold this view would naturally cite Confucius as their authority, though in actual fact nowhere did the Master expound a comprehensive theory of poetry, and our knowledge of his opinions on the subject is derived from isolated remarks he made about *The Book of Poetry*, to which he referred simply as *Poetry* or *The Three Hundred Poems*. It is doubtful if he ever formed a clearly defined concept of poetry as such, and even his remarks about *The Book of Poetry* seem to have varied in nature according to the circumstances in which they were made. Notwithstanding these reservations, we may still deduce from these remarks what Confucius's general views on poetry were. The following quotations from the *Analects* represent what he said about *The Book of Poetry* as a whole, apart from comments on specific passages.

The Three Hundred Poems may be summed up in one phrase: 'No evil thoughts'.

Let yourself be inspired by *Poetry*, confirmed by ritual, and perfected by music.

Though a man can recite *The Three Hundred Poems*, if he cannot carry out his duties when entrusted with affairs of state, and cannot answer questions on his own when sent on a mission abroad, what is the use of having studied the poems, no matter how many?

If you do not study *Poetry*, you will not be able to converse. (Said to his son.)

Poetry can serve to inspire emotion, to help your observation, to make you fit for company, to express your grievances, to teach you how to serve your father at home and your prince abroad, to enable you to learn the correct names of many birds, beasts, herbs, and trees.

It is clear from the above-quoted remarks that Confucius regarded *The Book of Poetry* not only as a means of exerting moral influence and of inspiring emotion but as a model of eloquence and a kind of thesaurus as well. His conception of poetry would therefore seem to be not entirely didactic. Indeed, some of these remarks may be considered the germs of theories other than that poetry is moral instruction.[1]

A little later, the *Preface to The Book of Poetry*, traditionally attributed to Confucius's disciple Pu Shang, better known as Tzŭ-hsia (507-400 B.C.), made a more definite statement of the didactic doctrine:

Nothing approaches *The Book of Poetry* in setting up standards of right and wrong, in moving Heaven and Earth, and in appealing to spirits and gods. The ancient kings used it to make permanent the tie between husband and wife, to perfect filial reverence, to deepen human relationships, to beautify moral instruction, and to improve the customs of the people.

This statement, with variations, has been repeated with monotonous regularity for centuries by scholars and critics. Poets, too, paid lip service to this doctrine, whether they made any effort to live up to it in practice or not. Tu Fu, for instance, wrote in a long poem that his youthful ambition had been to place his sovereign above the legendary sages, Emperors Yao and Shun, and to make the morals of the people pure once more. Even the egocentric Li Po lamented the sad decline of poetry since the end of the Han dynasty and professed a wish to follow in the footsteps of

---

[1] Cf. below, pp. 70 and 77.

Confucius and revive the tradition of *The Book of Poetry*. Po Chü-I, in his turn, deplored the fact that among the poems of Li Po and Tu Fu, only a small proportion described the sufferings of the people and pointed morals. To give more examples of such avowels of pious sentiments might become tedious. So, instead, I will simply summarize the main points made by those who subscribed to the didactic view.

First of all, poetry is regarded as a means to influence personal morality. To use the words of Shen Tê-ch'ien (1673–1769), a typical didactic critic, 'Poetry can regulate one's nature and emotion, and improve human relationships.' Like music, poetry is supposed to have a moderating influence, which can mould one's moral character to conform to the Confucian ideal of the golden mean (*chung yung*). Therefore, poetry should be 'moderate, gentle, sincere, and deep' (*wen jou tun hou*), as *The Book of Poetry* allegedly is. The first song in this anthology, commended by Confucius for expressing 'joy without licentiousness and grief without heart-rending', is held up by didactic critics as an ideal for all poetry.

Secondly, poetry should reflect the people's feelings towards the government and expose social evils. According to the *History of the Han Dynasty*, in ancient times there were officials sent out by the king to collect songs from the people so as to test public opinion. Whether this ancient Gallup poll really existed is doubtful, but its supposed existence is used by didactic critics as a proof that the original functions of poetry included political and social criticism. However, here too the poet should be moderate, 'showing grievances without being rebellious' (said of a section of *The Book of Poetry*). He should bring the people's sufferings to the notice of the ruler in the hope that the latter may be moved to mend his ways, but not incite rebellion. To achieve this aim, the poet should make use of allegory and satire, rather than openly attack the government. This is known as *feng chien*, or 'satirize and admonish'. Most of the poems, even obvious love songs, in *The Book of Poetry* and other ancient anthologies have been interpreted allegorically by Confucian critics to make them appear as if they fulfilled this function.

Another belief held by didactic critics is that whether concerned with personal morals or public issues, poetry should aspire to be *ya*. This word, which has come to mean 'elegant, refined', originally meant 'correct', and as an ideal for poetry, 'correctness' seems to refer both to the sentiments expressed and the way of expression. Vulgar and inordinate feelings, seditious thoughts, and extravagant language are equally abhorrent to those who seek 'correctness' in poetry.

So far we have been concerned with the question what poetry is, or ought to be. We may now turn to the question how one should write poetry. In reply to this question, didactic critics would advise one to imitate ancient poets. Shen Tê-ch'ien said, 'poetry that does not imitate the ancients is called "Wild Style".' In order to imitate ancient poets, one must of course study their works. We have seen that Confucius regarded *The Book of Poetry* as a manual of rhetoric among other things, and as time went on, the number of standard works to be studied grew ever greater, to become an immense repository of learning which would-be poets are advised to draw on. Moreover, one should read widely outside the field of poetry and display one's learning in one's poetry. To quote Shen Tê-ch'ien again, 'To use what is poetic in poetry is commonplace; it is only when you quote from the classics, the histories, and the philosophers in poetry that you can make it different from wild and groundless writings.'

Another means to help one to imitate the ancients is to pay attention to metrical rules. If one can manage to use metres in the same way as the ancient poets, then one's verse would at least bear some resemblance to the models. In this respect, the didactic critics have something in common with those others who regard poetry mainly as a kind of literary exercise. The latter will be discussed in Chapter 3.

Somewhat paradoxically, didactic critics, who advocate imitation, at the same time condemn artificiality and over-elaboration in poetry. Simplicity is their ideal. This is partly due to the fact that early poetry, especially poetry before the end of the Han dynasty, tends to have a simple style, and partly due to the ideals of moderation and correctness mentioned above. Therefore, poets of the Six Dynasties (222-589) and others are often criticized for their ornate and artificial style.

Finally, didactic critics judge poems more by their themes than by their style. For instance, Po Chü-I condemned some poets of the Six Dynasties not only for their style but for writing on such trivial themes as 'wind and snow, flowers and herbs' without using them for allegorical purposes. According to Po and other Moralists, frivolous themes are to be avoided, unless one treats them in such a way as to endow them with moral and political significance, so as to fulfil the function of 'satirizing and admonishing'.

2

THE INDIVIDUALIST VIEW:
POETRY AS
SELF-EXPRESSION

THE view that poetry is mainly an expression of personal emotions is at least as old as the didactic one, if not older. To the legendary sage Emperor Shun (traditional dates 2255–2205 B.C.) is attributed the remark, 'Poetry expresses the heart's wishes (*chih*)[1] in words; songs set words to music'. Confucius, as we have seen, observed that poetry could inspire emotion. And in the *Preface to The Book of Poetry*, side by side with the statement of the didactic doctrine quoted in the preceding chapter, we find the following:

> Poetry is where the heart's wishes go. What lies in the heart is 'wish', when expressed in words, it is 'poetry'. When an emotion stirs within one, one expresses it in words; finding this inadequate, one sighs over it; not content with this, one sings it in poetry; still not satisfied, one unconsciously dances with one's hands and feet.

Thus, both views—the didactic and the, for want of a better term, individualist—ran parallel in early Confucian writings on poetry. Later critics sometimes found difficulty in choosing between the two, or in trying to reconcile them. Liu Hsieh of the sixth century, one of the most important critics in Chinese literary history, may be taken as an example of the attempt to reconcile the

---

[1] A discussion on the meaning of this word will follow on p. 72.

two views. In his *magnum opus, Dragon Carvings of a Literary Mind* (*Wen-hsin Tiao-lung*), he writes:

> The Great Shun said, 'Poetry expresses the heart's wishes in words; songs set words to music'. This exposition by the sage has clearly shown the nature of poetry. Therefore, 'what lies in the heart is "wish", when expressed in words, it is "poetry".'

This is of course a mere re-statement of the view that poetry is an expression of the heart. However, he goes on to say,

> Poetry (*shih*) means 'to keep' (*ch'ih*). In other words, it is what *keeps* one's nature and emotion (in balance?). The *Three Hundred Poems* can be summed up in one phrase, 'No evil thoughts'. If one keeps this as a motto, it will have its proper effect.

Here he plays on the words *shih* 詩 ('poetry') and *ch'ih* 持 ('to keep'), and tries to turn the idea that poetry *expresses* one's nature and emotion into one that it keeps them in a balanced state (or perhaps preserves them in their innate state, the point not being made clear). He further confuses the issue by saying that one should *keep* (still playing on this word!) as one's moral ideal in poetry the phrase 'No evil thoughts'. In this way he hopes, somewhat naïvely, to effect a compromise between the two views. But no sooner has he done so than he reverts to the individualist one:

> A man is born with seven emotions, which are moved in response to external objects. It is only natural to be moved by external objects and to sing one's heart's wishes.

Now, he seems to have turned a complete circle and come back to where he started, after a vain effort to reconcile the individualist view with the didactic. It appears that at heart he is really inclined to the former, though he deems it desirable to bring in the didactic element as best he can, for in another chapter of the same book he emphasizes the importance of genuine emotion in poetry and condemns those who write for the sake of fine writing:

> Formerly, poets who wrote the songs in *The Book of Poetry* created literature for the sake of emotion, but the *literati* who composed 'expositions' (*Fu*) and 'odes' (*Sung*) manufactured emotion for the sake of literature. How so? *The Book of Poetry* was inspired by the dictates of the heart and long pent-up indignation; it expressed the emotions and nature of the poets, in order to satirize their rulers. This is what I call 'creating literature for the sake of emotion'. On the other hand, the followers of the various schools, who bore no great sorrow in their heart, displayed their talents and adorned their writings with

71

extravagance, in order to acquire reputation and fish for compliments. This is what I call 'manufacturing emotion for the sake of literature'. Therefore, what is written for the sake of expressing emotion is concise and true to life; what is written for the sake of literature is over-decorative and extravagant.

This is finely said, although even here he finds it necessary to drag in the moral element, which rather spoils his whole argument, for it is hard to see how an expression of one's emotion and nature will satirize and admonish one's ruler.

Other critics are more single-minded. They either stick to the extreme didactic view or to its opposite. The crux of the contention between these two opposing schools is their understanding of the character *chih* 志 (ancient form 㞢), which I have tentatively rendered as 'heart's wishes'. This character consists of a phonetic *chih* 之 (ancient form 㞢; 'to go') and a significant *hsin* 心 (ancient form 㣺; 'heart' or 'mind'). Hence the whole character is taken to mean 'where the heart (or mind) goes'. To the Moralists, *hsin* is 'mind', and 'where the mind goes' means 'will', 'mental inclination', or even 'ideal'. (The Neo-Confucian scholars of the Sung dynasty, for instance, identified *chih* with moral ideal.) In this way, poetry becomes an expression of one's moral ideal and mental inclinations. To the Individualists, *hsin* is 'heart', and 'where the heart goes' may be equated with 'heart's wishes', 'desires', or 'emotions'. Thus, poetry is an expression of one's heart. These two conflicting conceptions may be summarized in the following formulae:

The didactic conception:

> Poetry = expression of *chih*
> *Chih* = *hsin* + go
> *Hsin* = mind
> ∴ *Chih* = mental inclination, will, ideal.
> Poetry = expression of mental inclination, will, ideal.

The individualist conception:

> Poetry = expression of *chih*
> *Chih* = *hsin* + go
> *Hsin* = heart
> ∴ *Chih* = heart's wish, desire, emotion.
> Poetry = expression of heart's wish, desire, emotion.

The Individualist View: Poetry as Self-Expression

Of these two contradictory conceptions, the latter seems more likely to be the correct one. While it is true that the word *chih* could mean 'will', 'ambition', or 'ideal' in different contexts, and that the word *hsin* often means 'mind' rather than 'heart', it is clear that, in the passage from the *Preface to The Book of Poetry* quoted above, Tzu-hsia, or whoever wrote it, was thinking of 'heart' and 'emotion', not 'mind' and 'ideal', for the remark that 'poetry expresses the *chih*' is immediately followed by 'When an *emotion* stirs in one . . .'. One cannot help suspecting the Moralists of deliberately twisting the meaning of *chih* in order to make the saying 'Poetry expresses the *chih*', attributed to an ancient sage and therefore not to be dismissed, conform to the doctrine that poetry is concerned with moral teaching.

Another point on which the Moralists and the Individualists differ is the relation between poetry and one's emotion (*ch'ing*) and nature (*hsing*). The Moralists, while admitting poetry is concerned with these, emphasize the *effect* of poetry on them, thereby leaving unimpaired the doctrine that poetry should wield moral influence on one's character. The Individualists, on the other hand, emphasize the *expression* of these in poetry, whether the emotion and nature thus expressed are morally uplifting or not.

Two critics stand out among the Individualists: Chin Sheng-t'an (?–1661) and Yuan Mei (1716–1797). To the question what poetry is, Chin Sheng-t'an's answer is straightforward:

Poetry is nothing extraordinary; it is only the words which rise from the heart and lie at the tip of the tongue, and which everyone cannot help longing to utter. The scholars, making use of the ten thousand volumes they have studied thoroughly in their lifetime, cut such words into forms and embellish them with elegance. That poetry possesses forms and elegance is a thing the scholars boast about as due to the skill of which they alone are capable. As for its original nature, it is simply the words that, rising from everyone's heart and lying at the tip of his tongue, force themselves to be uttered, and not a thing the scholars can boast about as due to their special skill.

Yuan Mei's answer is similar:

Poetry is what expresses one's nature and emotion. It is enough to look no further than one's self (for the material of poetry). If its words move the heart, its colours catch the eye, its taste pleases the mouth, and its sound delights the ear, then it is good poetry.

From these remarks we can see that there are slight differences between Chin's conception of poetry and Yuan's, though their basic

73

outlook is the same. In the first place, poetry is to Chin Sheng-t'an an expression of emotions shared by all human beings, to Yuan Mei it is an expression of the poet's unique personality. Secondly, while the former is content to accept emotion as the be-all and end-all of poetry, the latter stresses the aesthetic and sensuous elements of poetry as well. That is why Yuan Mei advocates what he calls 'native sensibility' (*hsing ling* 性 靈) in addition to 'nature and emotion' (*hsing ch'ing*). This concept of Native Sensibility implies that while a poet should preserve the natural feelings of a child ('a poet is one who has not lost the heart of a child', says Yuan), he should at the same time possess a high degree of sensibility ingrained in his nature. What makes a poet different from others who may have equally strong natural feelings is his sensibility (*ling*); what makes one poet different from another poet is the special kind of sensibility which forms part of his nature (*hsing*). In this, Yuan shows more discrimination and insight than Chin. Whereas Chin merely recognizes what may provide the impulse for writing poetry, Yuan realizes that an individual sensibility is needed as well as emotion.

As to how one should write poetry, both critics would advise one to rely on spontaneous feelings rather than technique or learning or imitation. Chin says:

How can the number of words and lines in a poem be limited? Poetry is a sudden cry from the heart, which comes to everyone, even a woman or a child, in the morning or at mid-night. Now, suppose here is a new-born baby whose eyes cannot yet turn and whose fists cannot yet stretch, but who, extending its arms and twisting its feet, utters a sound from its mouth. When I look at it carefully, I find this is really poetry. There is no one in the world, who, not having been moved in the heart, will utter a sound from his mouth; nor is there anyone who, having been moved in the heart, will remain silent. What moves the heart and is uttered from the mouth is called poetry. That is why Tzǔ-hsia said, 'What lies in the heart is "wish"; when expressed in words, it is "poetry".' . . . Where the heart goes, a wish is formed; where words go, poetry then comes into being. Therefore, there is no poetry that does not arise out of a cry from the mouth. The T'ang people formulated metrical rules and forced everyone to write eight lines of five or seven syllables. But if every piece must have eight lines and every line must have five or seven syllables, how can that be called poetry? In fact, I know that the Regulated Verse of the T'ang poets does not lie beyond what everybody in the world utters from his mouth. How do I know this? I have come to know it after having analysed their poems.

To avoid any misunderstanding, it should be pointed out that it is not so much the T'ang poets as their imitators that Chin is criticizing. Though he blames the T'ang poets for having formulated the rules of Regulated Verse, he admits that they have succeeded in expressing natural emotion in spite of metrical rules. It is those who merely imitate the T'ang poets in versification but have no emotion to express that Chin is condemning. Similarly, Yuan Mei says:

> Poetry is what expresses one's nature and emotion. . . . How can it be restricted to one or two rimes?

And again:

> As long as you have your nature and emotion, you will have metre and rules. Metre and rules do not lie beyond one's nature and emotion.

Both critics emphasize sincerity on the part of the poet and emotional response on the part of the reader. Chin says:

> In writing poetry, one must express what is felt sincerely in the heart and what is felt in common with others in the heart. It is because poetry expresses what is felt sincerely in the heart that tears can fall in response to one's brush-strokes; and it is because it expresses what is felt in common with others in the heart that it can make one's readers shed tears in response to one's utterance. Now if one only writes the four middle lines (of an eight-line poem in Regulated Verse), is that what is felt sincerely in the heart, or felt in common with others in the heart? If the T'ang poets had also written only the four middle lines of their poems, how could we even now shed tears while reading them?

Likewise, Yuan condemns writing for the sake of writing, when one has not been compelled by some emotion to write:

> I like best Chou Li-yuan's remark on poetry: Poetry is what expresses my emotions. Therefore, if I want to write, I do; if not, I don't. There has never been anyone forcing and exhorting me to write poetry.

In conjunction with his condemnation of writing without genuine emotion, Yuan is particularly averse to the excessive use of allusions, a common fault among Chinese poets. He criticized Wang Shih-chen, whom we shall discuss in Chapter 4, for being 'more concerned with elegance of style than emotion':

> Everywhere he went, he must write a poem, and in every poem there must be allusions. From this we can gather that his emotions are not genuine.

Once more he says,

A man who knows many allusions but does not use them is like one who has power and influence but does not show them off.

These remarks may not sound original or startling to Western readers, but taken in their historical context they represent independent and courageous opinions. They show a fresh understanding of poetry as a means of self-expression, not a form of moral propaganda or academic exercise.

3

THE TECHNICAL VIEW: POETRY AS LITERARY EXERCISE

I⊤ will be recalled that Confucius thought of poetry as, among other things, an aid to one's vocabulary and eloquence.[1] This may be considered the germ of the view that poetry is mainly concerned with book-learning and sheer verbal ingenuity—in other words, a kind of literary exercise where technique reigns supreme. Such a technical view of poetry is not always explicitly professed, but often implied in practice. For instance, writers of lengthy and pedantic 'expositions' (*Fu*) of the Han dynasty are generally more interested in displaying their erudition than in expressing any emotion or moral ideals, and since the Sung dynasty many literary men have written verses prompted by neither serious moral motives nor strong emotional urge. To them, writing verse in classical metres is an elegant pastime and a way to prove that one is cultured, as writing Latin verse used to be a sign of culture for English gentlemen. Such literary gentlemen would gather together at regular meetings, compose verse on given subjects, and echo (*ho*) each other's poems using the same metre and rimes. It is obvious that practices such as these are hardly conducive to spontaneous creative writing. That is why both Yuan Mei and Wang Shih-chen objected to echoing poems. But the practice is by no means dead even now among older Chinese literary men.

[1] See above, p. 66.

77

It is not difficult to guess what answers one would get from adherents of the technical view to the question how to write poetry. They advocate imitation of earlier poets and mastery of the technique of versification. The Moralists too, as we have seen, hold such views, but apart from the even greater preoccupation with technical details on the part of the Technicians, there are other differences between the two schools. In the first place, the Moralists hold up very ancient poems (works of Han and earlier periods) with their simple language as models, while the Technicians usually imitate later poets, particularly those of the T'ang dynasty. For example, during the Sung dynasty various schools of poets were formed, each devoting itself to the task of imitating a particular T'ang poet: the Hsiang-shan School imitated Po Chü-I; the Hsi-k'un School, Li Shang-yin; the Late T'ang School, Chia Tao; the Ch'ang-li School, Han Yü. Consequently, followers of the didactic doctrine aim at simplicity, while those of the Technical School often recommend a highly involved and obscure style.

Among holders of the Technical view, there is a shift of emphasis between imitation of previous poets and the technique of versification. Some regard imitation as of paramount importance; others pay more attention to details of versification. The Sung poet Huang T'ing-chien (1045–1105) may be called the archimitator. He mainly imitated two poets: T'ao Ch'ien and Tu Fu, and he frankly admitted the necessity for imitation:

> Ideas for poetry are inexhaustible but human talent is limited. To use a limited talent to chase inexhaustible ideas is a task that not even T'ao Ch'ien and Tu Fu could fulfil.

Therefore, for lesser geniuses, imitation is the only sensible thing to do. Huang developed two methods of imitation, which he called 'Changing the Bone' (*huan ku* 換骨) and 'Evolving from the Embryo' (*to t'ai* 奪胎). The former means imitating the idea while using different words; the latter means imitating the words while using a somewhat different idea. To paraphrase: the former is to put old wine in a new bottle, the latter, new wine in an old bottle. Thus, imitation was raised to the status of a fine art. It must be admitted that the result can be quite admirable at times, though the principle can hardly be defended.

One critic who puts form and versification above imitation in importance is Li Tung-yang (1447–1516) of the Ming dynasty. He says:

> In writing poetry, one must have a perfect eye and one must have a perfect ear. The eye is concerned with form, the ear with sound.

To him, verse forms and metrical rules are the very *raison d'être* of poetry:

> What makes poetry different from prose is that it possesses regulated sounds and can be recited.

It is necessary, he insists, to keep each verse form distinct from the others:

> Ancient Verse and Regulated Verse are different forms; each must be written according to its own form before it can be considered proper. Occasionally one might use a touch of Ancient Verse in Regulated Verse, but on no account should one introduce a note of Regulated Verse into Ancient Verse.

And he admires poets like Tu Fu not for their thoughts and feelings but for their skilful manipulation of tones and pauses and their subtle use of particles and verbs. In this he is by no means alone. A scholar of the Ch'ing period, named Chou Ch'un, devoted years to the compilation of a work on alliteration and riming compounds in Tu Fu's poetry—a labour of love which to the irreverent seems more like a love of labour, and which is reminiscent of the works of some Western scholars who counted the number of 'feminine endings' in Shakespeare's blank verse.

In one respect Li Tung-yang stands apart from other critics of the Technical School: he is against imitation. According to him, a poet should read widely and apply his learning to harmonious and rhythmic language. If so, one's poetry can be recited and sung, repeated by contemporaries and remembered by posterity. There is no need to imitate any particular school or period, as long as one's poetry is musical. In other words, poetry is nothing but learning embodied in musical language.

To most of the other critics of this school, imitation is of great importance, for it is conceived of as a means to achieve perfect mastery of technique. Another critic of the Ming period, and one with a rather similar name, Li Meng-yang (1472–1528), states:

> In writing poetry, one must imitate Tu Fu. His poetry is like a perfect circle that can dispense with the compasses, or a perfect square that can dispense with the rulers.

It is because Tu Fu has completely assimilated metrical rules in his poetry that it appears so perfect, and by imitating him one can in fact learn all the rules of versification—such are the implications of Li Meng-yang's statement. He reiterates similar ideas elsewhere:

> Words must have methods and rules before they can fit and harmonize with musical laws, just as circles and squares must fit with compasses and rulers. The ancients used rules, which were not invented by them but really created by Nature. Now, when we imitate the ancients, we are not imitating them but really imitating the natural laws of things.

This is an ingenious and plausible defence of imitation, for it identifies imitation with learning metrical rules, which are in turn identified with the natural laws of rhythm and euphony.

These ideas are echoed by a later critic Weng Fang-kang (1733–1818), who writes in his essay on 'Poetic Method':

> The fundamental principles of poetic methods do not originate with oneself; they are like rivers flowing into the sea, and one must trace their sources back to the ancients. As for the infinitely varied applications of poetic methods, from such major considerations as the structural principles down to such details as the grammatical nature of a word, the tone of a syllable, and the points of continuation, transition, and development—all these one must learn from the ancients. Only so can one realize that everything is done according to rules and in consonance with the laws of music and that one cannot do as one likes to the slightest degree.

This uncompromising attitude is also shown in his two essays on 'Spirit and Tone', in which he advances his theory of 'flesh texture' (*chi-li* 肌 理) as an antidote against that of 'spirit and tone', a theory evolved by Wang Shih-chen, which we shall discuss in the next chapter. Weng Fang-kang claims that what other critics call 'spirit and tone' are in fact nothing but the 'flesh texture' of poetry, and that one should seek poetic excellence first of all in the texture of words:

> If one realizes that one should seek it in the flesh texture, then all the time one will be afraid of not following the rules and standards precisely. And why must one talk about 'spirit and tone'?

This may be regarded as the Technical view pushed to its logical conclusion.

4

THE INTUITIONALIST
VIEW: POETRY AS
CONTEMPLATION

SINCE the Sung dynasty there have been a few critics who did
not subscribe to any of the views on poetry mentioned in the
foregoing chapters, and who, though a minority, made significant
contributions to the criticism of poetry in Chinese. Their concep-
tion of poetry, if put in modern terms, would be: poetry is an
embodiment of the poet's contemplation of the world and of his
own mind. This school of criticism arose under the influence of
Ch'an, or, to give its Japanese name by which it is better known in
the West, Zen Buddhism, and its first important spokesman was
Yen Yü of the thirteenth century. Although other critics before
him had occasionally applied Zen terms to poetry, Yen was the
first to discuss poetry consistently in terms of Zen, and the one
who has had the greatest influence on later critics. It is therefore
convenient to begin with a brief exposition of Yen Yü's ideas on
poetry.

In his view, the poet, like the follower of Zen, should seek to
attain to a calm contemplative state of mind. When one has
achieved this, one can then hope to capture the spirit (*shen*)of life,
of Nature, in one's poetry. Yen writes:

> The ultimate excellence of poetry lies in one thing: entering the
> spirit. If poetry can succeed in doing this, it will have reached the limit
> and cannot be surpassed.

81

What he means by 'entering the spirit', I think, is to enter imaginatively into the life of things and embody their essence, their spirit, in one's poetry. In other words, the poet should not assert his own personality but assume a 'Negative Capability' (to borrow Keats's term), so as to identify himself with the object of his contemplation. That is why Yen Yü, while admitting that poetry is concerned with emotion, disapproves of any excessive display of it:

> The worst of them (modern poets) even scream and growl, which is against the principle of magnanimity (as exemplified by *The Book of Poetry*). These people are using abusive language as poetry. When poetry has deteriorated to such a state, it can be truly called a disaster.

For him, ideal poetry is that which forms a reflection, an image, of the world, and which resembles Nature in its freedom from personal emotion and traces of conscious artistry. It should be like 'echoes in the air, reflection of the moon in water, or an image in the mirror'. Thus, these symbols originally used by Buddhists to illustrate the illusory nature of all existence become for him descriptions of a kind of poetry which is elusive and indefinable in quality.

In direct contrast to the Moralists, Yen asserts:

> Poetry involves a different kind of talent, which is not concerned with books; it involves a different kind of meaning, which is not concerned with principles.

He therefore condemns pedantry and imitation in poetry:

> Modern scholars use literary language as poetry; use learnings as poetry; use discussion as poetry. Are their works not skilful? Yes, but they lack that which 'leaves three lingering echoes after each note'. Moreover, in their works, they must always use allusions, while disregarding inspiration. Every word they use must be derived from someone; every rime they use must have some precedent. Yet when one reads them over and over again from beginning to end, one does not know what they are aiming at.

It is clear from the above-quoted remarks that Yen Yü regards poetry neither as moral teaching nor as literary exercise, nor even as self-expression, but as an embodiment of the poet's vision of the world, or to put it the other way round, of the world reflected through the poet's consciousness.

Among later critics influenced by Yen Yü, I shall mention three, who all happen to bear the same surname: Wang Fu-chih (1619–

1692), Wang Shih-chen (1634–1711), and Wang Kuo-wei (1877–1927). All three agree that poetry is not only concerned with expression of emotion (*ch'ing* 情) but with reflection of external 'scene' (*ching* 景). The best kind of poetry is that which effects a fusion between emotion and scene. According to Wang Fu-chih,

> 'Emotion' and 'scene' are called by two different names, but in fact they cannot be separated. Those who can work wonders in poetry can unite the two naturally and leave no boundary line; those who are skilful, can reveal an emotion in a scene and a scene in an emotion.

He further says:

> Though emotion and scene differ in that one lies in the heart and the other in things, they actually engender each other.

Moreover, it is not enough to embody emotion and scene in poetry; one must also catch the spirit of things:

> If one cherishes emotions and can convey them; if one appreciates a scene and is moved in the heart; if one understands the nature of things and can capture their spirit; then one will naturally find inspired and lively lines, and reach the state of natural marvel that shows no signs of technical skill.

To the idea of 'spirit', Wang Shih-chen added that of 'tone' (*yun* 韻). Since he often mentioned the two together, they have been taken to mean one thing: spiritual harmony. But I think they refer to two things: 'spirit' refers to the essence of things, while 'tone' refers to a personal style, idiom, or flavour in poetry. That this was how Wang Shih-chen understood these two words may be seen from the following facts. In his collected remarks on poetry, the *Tai-ching-t'ang Shih-hua*, there is one section under the heading 'Entering the Spirit' (*ju shen*), a phrase first used by Yen Yü, as we have seen; and all the lines quoted in this section are descriptions of 'scenes'. It is clear, then, that by 'spirit' Wang Shih-chen meant capturing the essence of external objects. As for 'tone', we can see that he used the word to mean a personal flavour in poetry from the fact that he quoted with approval a remark made by the Sung poet, composer, and critic Chiang K'uei (1163?–1203?):

> The poetry of each master has its own flavour, just as each of the twenty-four modes of music has its own 'tone', on which the music depends for its character. Imitators, though their words may resemble the master's, have lost the tone.

We can further see that Wang Shih-chen attached some importance to the individual quality of poetry from these words:

> Ancient poets like T'ao Ch'ien, Hsieh Ling-yun, Wang Wei, Tu Fu and Wei Ying-wu all left poetry behind them. Now, when we compare their poetry with their lives, we find the poetry of each is just like the man himself.

In this he shows some affinity with the Individualists, but his whole approach to poetry is quite different. He is interested in achieving a personal tone, a literary *persona*, rather than expressing his personality and intimate feelings, as Yuan Mei is. The latter, we remember, criticized Wang Shih-chen for his lack of genuine emotions.[1] It would be truer to say that Wang Shih-chen is not primarily concerned with expressing emotion. His ideal is to embody in poetry the spirit (*shen*) of life, as distilled through an individual sensibility, so that this poetry will acquire a personal 'tone' (*yun*).

From the concepts of 'emotion and scene' and 'spirit and tone', Wang Kuo-wei derived his theory of 'worlds' in poetry. The term I have translated as 'world', *ching-chieh* 境界, is itself a translation of the Sanskrit word *visaya*, which in Buddhist terminology means 'sphere' or 'spiritual domain'. Wang Kuo-wei was not the first to apply it to poetry, but he was the first to use it systematically and to give it something like a definition:

> The 'world' does not refer to scenes and objects only; joy, anger, sadness, and happiness also form a world in the human heart. Therefore poetry that can describe true scenes and true emotions may be said to 'have a world'; otherwise it may be said 'not to have a world'.

This 'world' is in fact a fusion of emotion and scene, and the concept is obviously derived from Wang Fu-chih's 'emotion and scene', though now given a new name. Wang Kuo-wei distinguishes those who 'create worlds' in poetry from those who only 'describe' them:

> There are some (poets) who create worlds, and others who describe worlds. This is the origin of the distinction between Idealism and Realism. Yet the two are hard to separate, for the worlds created by a great poet are always in accord with Nature, and those described by him always approach the ideal.

[1] See p. 75.

84

The Intuitionalist View: Poetry as Contemplation

This distinction I propose to discuss later, in Part III.[1] Meanwhile, we can turn our attention to the question how one should write poetry.

To this question, Yen Yü would reply: depend on inspiration and intuitive apprehension. The greatness of the major T'ang poets, he says, lies solely in their 'inspired interest' (*hsing ch'ü* 興 趣), which leaves no traces of technique. He further states:

In general, the way of Zen lies in intuitive apprehension, so does the way of poetry. For instance, Meng Hao-jan's learning was inferior to Han Yü's, yet his poetry was superior. This was due to his complete reliance on intuitive apprehension. Only through this can one be one's true self and show one's natural colours.

This is followed by the three Wangs, who also emphasize intuition and condemn imitation and pedantry. As we have already seen, Wang Fu-chih maintains that as long as one can capture the spirit of things, one will naturally find inspired and lively lines. He goes on to say:

If, on the other hand, one merely seeks skilfulness in one's lines, one's nature and emotion will have gone astray first, and there will be no life in one's poetry.

Similarly, Wang Shih-chen stresses the importance of inspiration, which he calls 'sudden illumination' (*tun wu* 頓 悟), another term borrowed from Zen Buddhism. To him, the art of poetry is a secret that cannot be communicated in words but will dawn on one in a flash of intuitive apprehension. Drawing analogies between writing poetry and other forms of discipline, he says:

The Maiden of Yueh, when discussing the art of swordsmanship with Kou-chien, said, 'I did not receive it from anyone; I just suddenly got it.' Ssǔ-ma Hsiang-ju, when asked about the art of writing the 'exposition' (*Fu*), replied, 'The mind of a *Fu*-writer can be achieved from within but cannot be conveyed in words.' The Zen Master Yun-men said to his disciples, 'You do not try to remember your own words but try to remember mine. Are you going to sell me in the future?' All these remarks have hit the secret of poetry.

The implications of this passage are not far to seek: that writing poetry is not a thing one can master by sheer study, that inspiration will come to the deserving when the moment is ripe, that mere imitation is of no use. However, Wang Shih-chen and the other

[1] See below, p. 99.

critics of this school are not against study as such; what they recommend is that one should completely assimilate one's learning and reveal no trace of it in poetry. That is why Yen Yü himself, after remarking that poetry is not concerned with books, adds, 'but unless one reads widely, one will not reach the limit of excellence'. That is also why Wang Shih-chen, though against pedantry in general, does not object to the use of allusions, as long as their origins are not made obvious. Yuan Mei, as we have seen, criticized Wang Shih-chen for using too many allusions, but there is really no inconsistency between Wang's theory and practice. After all, the two ways of achieving enlightenment, 'sudden illumination' and 'gradual cultivation' (*chien hsiu* 漸 修), are mutually complementary rather than mutually exclusive, for unless one has been cultivating one's mind, one will not be ready to receive the sudden illumination even when it comes. The same is true when applied to poetry: one cannot be inspired to write great poetry without first having learnt to read and write. What the Intuitionalists object to is not learning as such, but undigested learning and pedantry that parade as poetry. Therefore, Wang Shih-chen objects to the practice of echoing poems with the same rimes, and for similar reasons Wang Kuo-wei holds up to ridicule those critics who recommend the use of hackneyed metaphors such as 'red rain' for peach blossoms.

Another point made by the Intuitionalists is that poetry should try to produce its effect by suggestion rather than direct statement or description. Yen Yü said that 'poetry that does not concern itself with principles nor falls into the trammel of words is the best', and that great poetry 'has limited words but unlimited meaning'. It follows that the poet should not heap up too many realistic details but attempt to capture the spirit of things with a few quick strokes of the brush. As an example of the dislike of excessive realism, we may mention that Wang Shih-chen defended some T'ang poets who brought together in their poems rivers and mountains actually miles apart, by saying that what matters is the inspiration of the moment, not factual details.

In short, critics of the Intuitionalist School share a common basic conception of poetry. Whether they call it 'spirit and tone', 'emotion and scene', or 'world', they agree that the essence of poetry lies in its embodiment of the external world as reflected through the poet's mind, as well as its revelation of the internal world of feeling. They all stress the importance of intuition and inspiration, while condemning pedantry, imitation, and pre-occupation with technique. In the last respect they are in sympathy with the Individualists, but their fundamental attitude is different in that they are not content with an expression of one's own personality but seek to convey a vision of the world.

PART III

Towards a Synthesis

I

POETRY AS EXPLORATION
OF WORLDS AND OF
LANGUAGE

Iɴ presenting the views of various Chinese critics in the pre-
ceding part, I have on the whole refrained from making critical
comments, though where my predilections and sympathies lie has
inevitably been revealed here and there. It is now time to consider
these views in a critical light and see if it is possible to effect a
synthesis among them, with modifications and additional ideas of
my own. In doing so, I shall in fact also clarify my own position
as a critic, for criticism, including and perhaps most of all
criticism of criticisms, cannot help being subjective in the final
analysis, so that in criticizing other critics one is bound to commit
oneself to certain convictions and points of view. However, as
long as the reader is aware where the critic he is reading stands
and where he himself stands, it matters little whether they agree or
not, because a communication between two minds has been
established, which may turn out to be fruitful.

It may be remarked here, in passing, that while discussing the
various schools of Chinese critics I have resisted the temptation
to draw facile analogies with European critics and to label the
Chinese critics with names of Western origin. It would have been
easy to dub the four schools I discussed as 'Classicists', 'Roman-
ticists', 'Formalists', and 'Symbolists' respectively, but to have
done so would have been misleading. In the first place, some of

these terms are vague enough in popular usage, carrying different implications and associations, flattering or derogatory according to the writer. However, when confined to their historical context, they can still be forced to mean something definite, whereas if we applied them to Chinese critics, they would lose all their terms of reference. Secondly, though the Chinese critics I discussed show some affinities with certain Western critics, there are many differences too. For example, the Individualists resemble the European Romanticists in their emphasis on self-expression, but they do not exhibit the kind of political and moral idealism often professed by the latter. Again, the Intuitionalists have some affinities with the Symbolists in their attempt to break down the barrier between the external world and the internal world, but the latter's preoccupation with verbal details and auditory effects bring them closer to the Chinese Technicians. It is therefore safer not to use any Western terms but to be content with such *ad hoc* labels as 'Moralists', 'Individualists', 'Technicians', and 'Intuitionalists', awkward and unwieldy as some of these may be.

Let us now consider each school in turn. The Moralists, whose counterparts in the West are not hard to find from Plato down to the present day, make the basic mistake of confusing the possible motives and effects of poetry with poetry itself. While one may be prompted by moral, political, or social motives to write a poem, these alone will not make one a poet. Whatever it is one wishes to convey—be it moral ideals, social grievances, or political views —one has to do so in words, and unless one has mastered the use of words in poetic forms, all the rest is of no use. Moreover, whatever one's motives, the act of writing poetry is not a moral, political, or social act, but a personal creative act involving one's emotional and intellectual powers. It is therefore absurd to criticize poetry on non-literary grounds.

Similarly, poetry may have effects on one's morals or political views, but such effects cannot determine its value as poetry. A reader has the right to *object to* a poem on political, moral, or even personal grounds, but no right to *condemn it as a bad poem* on the same grounds. To judge the literary value of a poem by its theme is as naïve as to judge a picture by its 'subject': it is tantamount to saying that any picture representing the Madonna or Buddha, however badly painted, is a better picture than one depicting a prostitute or a beggar.

In short, where the Moralists go wrong is to apply non-artistic standards to works of art. Or, to use the terminology of R. G. Collingwood, they confuse 'magic' with 'art'. Of course I do not mean that non-artistic standards of value are not important, only that they cannot be used to assess artistic values. It is the duty of the literary critic to assess literary values; but he should leave it to the readers themselves to relate these with other systems of values.

As for the Moralists' answer to the question how one should write poetry, since it is largely similar to that given by the Technicians, we will defer criticism till we come to the latter.

The Individualists, while recognizing that poetry is a form of self-expression, tend to commit an error similar to that of the Moralists, by identifying the *impulse* to write poetry with poetry itself. They stress, rightly, that a poet should have genuine emotion, but they often fail to see that emotion as such, no matter how strong and genuine, is not poetry. It is true that everyone is a *potential* poet, but it is absurd to pretend, as Chin Sheng-t'an does, that everyone, even a crying baby, *is* a poet. Even Yuan Mei's 'native sensibility' is still not enough: a person may have great sensibility without being able to express it in poetic language.

Secondly, they do not seem to consider whether all emotions are worth expressing in poetry. In other words, they do not adopt a critical attitude to their own experience. This indiscriminate attitude may result, as indeed it has in the case of Yuan Mei's own poetry, in superficiality and triviality.

Thirdly, their conception of poetry is too narrow, being confined to an expression of emotion and personality only. This leaves no room for purely intellectual reflections and the poet's response to the external world.

Finally, in their answer to the question how to write poetry, they again rely too much on emotion. Though it is desirable that a poet should have spontaneous feelings, he may not be able to express them in adequate poetic language. One can sympathize with the Individualists in their objection to imitation and pedantry, but one has to face the fact that spontaneous feelings do not automatically find their own poetic expression, for which a natural gift for words as well as acquired verbal skill is necessary.

While the Individualists neglect the importance of words, the

Towards a Synthesis

Technicians go to the other extreme by concentrating their attention on words and versification to the virtual exclusion of everything else. They are so busy worrying *how* to say things that they seem to forget to ask *what* to say. This is surely putting the cart before the horse.

Both the Technicians and the Moralists rely too much on imitation, not realizing that ancient poets only achieved their excellence after experimenting with language, and that incessant further experiments are needed. They fail to see that the best one can hope for in imitating ancient poets is to produce fake antiques, and that even if one could write like Tu Fu, it would not be right, for the simple reason that one is not Tu Fu and therefore should not speak with his voice.

The Intuitionalists I find most interesting, though there is room for improvement in their theories too. The concept of 'world' is a useful one, if we enlarge it to a greater extent, as I shall try to do below. The recognition that poetry is not confined to personal feelings frees it from egoistic fetters, but on the other hand there is a tendency on the part of the Intuitionalists to mystify and rarefy poetry, so that it appears to embody only a remote inaccessible world of pure contemplation. This too needs modification. Again, in advising one to rely on intuition in order to write poetry, they are indulging in mystification and obscurantism. Though it may be true that the nature of poetic genius is ultimately indefinable and inexplicable, it is unnecessary to make the writing of poetry sound like a mysterious and supernatural activity. After all, to write good poetry one needs conscious art as well as natural gift, call it 'intuition', 'inspiration', or what you will.

Having thus considered the various schools of critics, I will now proceed to develop my own view of poetry, which contains elements drawn from some of the critics discussed above, and from my own reflections.

To begin with, we have to reconsider the definition of 'world' in poetry. Wang Kuo-wei, we recall, defined it as consisting of 'emotion' and 'scene'.[1] This certainly applies to a great deal of poetry, Chinese or Western. A poem which seeks to convey emotion without any description of external scene may, in rare cases, achieve a kind of sublime simplicity, like Shakespeare's

[1] See p. 84.

94

> So long as men can breathe or eyes can see,
> So long lives this, and this gives life to thee

or Emily Dickinson's

> Parting is all we know of heaven
> And all we need of hell

or Guillaume Apollinaire's

> Vienne la nuit, sonne l'heure,
> Les jours s'en vont, je demeure.

But more often it will sink into sheer bathos, like Shelley's 'I die, I faint, I fail', or 'O World! O Life! O Time!' On the other hand, a poem which consists entirely of description of scene without any emotion can at best be skilful verse but can hardly be considered genuine poetry. Many Chinese 'expositions' (*Fu*) fall into this category and are condemned by Liu Hsieh for that reason.[1] It appears, therefore, that most poetry involves expression of emotion as well as description of external scene. When we read a poem closely, we often find it difficult, if not impossible, to separate the emotion from the scene. For example, T. S. Eliot's *Preludes* are superficially descriptions of city scenes, yet how effectively do they convey the feelings of boredom, depression, and disgust! Conversely, words explicitly emotive can also help to depict a scene. For instance, in

> That time of year thou mayst in me behold,
> When yellow leaves, or none, or few, do hang
> Upon those boughs which shake against the cold,
> Bare ruin'd choirs where late the sweet birds sang,

the images used by the poet to express his sadness at growing old at the same time paint an imaginary scene. Thus, the scene in a poem need not be actual: the images used by the poet to body forth his emotion also constitute a scene of their own, though of an imaginary order. As a matter of fact, the actual and imaginary scenes often merge into each other, such as in Baudelaire's lines

> Quand vers toi mes désires partent en caravane,
> Tes yeux sont la citerne où boivent mes ennuis.

Here, the image of clear water where the tired travellers drink, while creating an imaginary scene, also contributes to the descrip-

---

[1] See above, p. 71.

tion of the purity and depth of the woman's eyes, which form part of the actual scene. Simultaneously these lines also serve to give body to the poet's emotions: his desire for the woman addressed to, his weariness of life, his longing for rest and consolation. Lines like these are both expressive and descriptive: they convey certain emotions and evoke a scene, real or imaginary, at the same time.

However, if we regard a fusion of emotion and scene as the definition of 'world' in poetry, it would be difficult to fit into this definition poems devoted to narrative of events or purely intellectual speculation. It would be more satisfactory, therefore, if we re-defined 'world' as a synthesis of the external and the internal aspects of life, the former including not only natural objects and scenes but events and action, the latter including not only emotion but thought, memory, sensation, fantasy. In other words, a 'world' in poetry is at once a reflection of the poet's external environment and an expression of his total consciousness. Each poem embodies a world of its own, be it great or small, remote or familiar, but as long as the poetry is genuine, it will transport us into its special world, to enable us to see certain things, to feel certain emotions, to ponder on certain aspects of life, to experience in our imagination a state of being which we may or may not have experienced in real life.

Furthermore, we must stress that poetry does not merely *describe* different worlds, as if they were static, but *explores* them. For a poem is not a dead record of a past experience, but a living process of blending a past experience with the present experience of writing or reading the poem. (After all, what separate existence has 'a poem' apart from the process of being created by the poet and re-created by the reader?) A poet does not take an experience as the 'content' of his poem and pour it into a 'form'; he is prompted by some experience, be it an emotion, a thought, or an event, to write, and while he is searching for the right words, the right pattern of sounds and sequence of images, the original experience is transformed into something new—the poem. When the reader reads it, the process is repeated in his mind, and the world of that poem is re-created.

The above remarks imply that poetry is not only an exploration of external and internal worlds but also an exploration of the language in which it is written. While the original experience is undergoing transformation as the poet searches for the right words, an exploration of the possibilities of language is proceeding at the same time. Whatever the world the poet is exploring, his immediate concern is with words, with the 'intolerable wrestle with words and meanings'. Thus, poetry is seen to be a double exploration, and the poet's task is a double one: to find adequate words for new worlds of experience and to find new words for old familiar worlds. Some emotional worlds are universal and as old as mankind, such as those of love, hate, the joy of life and the fear of death, yet they may be experienced in different ways and in various degrees of intensity, and hence require different ways of expression. On the other hand, some ways of thinking or modes of feeling may be peculiar to a nation, an age, or even a particular social and cultural *milieu*. These constitute new worlds of experience and demand expression too. So, the poet's task is not only to say something for the first time, but also to say for the thousand and first time, in a different way, what has been said a thousand times already. It is this constant need to explore the possibilities of language that accounts for the existence of various verse forms and poetic devices. This was realized by the great scholar Ku Yen-wu of the seventeenth century:

> The reason why poetry changes its form from age to age is that there is something which makes change inevitable. The literary form of an age, when it has been followed for a long time, no longer allows everyone to say the same things over and over again in it. Now, after a thousand years, can we still take the hackneyed expressions of the ancients and call them poetry?

Later, Wang Kuo-wei echoed this:

> When a literary form has been current for a long time and used by many, it naturally becomes hackneyed. An independent-minded writer, finding it hard to say anything original in it, will turn away and evolve a new form to set himself free. This is the reason why each literary form flourishes for a time and finally declines.

Side by side with this search for new verse forms goes on the attempt to capture, with ever greater precision, nuances of meaning, subtle shades of feeling, exquisite and elusive moods, in words charged with implications and associations. The Chinese poets, like their European brethren, have also been attempting for centuries to give 'un sens plus pure aux mots de la tribu'. This attempt became increasingly conscious as the history of Chinese poetry developed: instead of expressing their thoughts and feelings in simple direct language, as the early anonymous poets had done, later poets were inclined to express themselves in an oblique manner, by means of imagery, symbolism, and allusions. Such explorations in the use of language on the part of the poets necessitate a great deal of linguistic analysis on our part as critics. But before undertaking any analysis let us return to the concept of poetry as a double exploration and consider its practical implications in criticism.

Since poetry is an exploration of different worlds and of language, it follows that in judging a poem we should apply two major criteria. On the one hand, we should ask, 'Does this poem explore a world of its own, and if so, what kind of world is it?' On the other hand, we should ask, 'Does it break new grounds in the use of language?' Upon the answers to these questions depends our judgement on whether the poem in question is genuine or fake, good or bad, 'great' or merely 'good'.

To answer the question whether a poem explores any particular world, we have to ask further subsidiary questions: 'Dc the external and the internal aspects of life form one homogeneous whole in the poem? Is the external world consistently observed in the light of some inner experience, or, alternatively, does the inner experience emerge naturally out of the external environment? Do the physical details build up a coherent picture in consonance with the inner experience, or are they a mechanically piled-up mess that falls to pieces on analysis?' These questions can be answered by anyone with disciplined sensibility and sufficient experience in reading poetry.

The next question to ask is: 'What kind of world does this poem lead us into?' Of course, it would be as childish to think one poem better than another because it has a 'greater' world as to think a landscape superior to a still life because mountains are bigger than apples. Nevertheless, in dealing with individual poems, and still more in dealing with the whole corpus of a poet's works, it is relevant to ask if we are brought into new worlds, higher spheres of thought, greater depths of feeling, wider fields of vision, or merely introduced to worlds already familiar to us. It seems to me that the difference between great and lesser poetry is that the former leads us into new worlds and therefore enlarges our sensibility, while the latter re-creates for us familiar worlds and therefore only confirms our own experience.[1] The former surprises us and even shocks us at times, before finally convincing us of its truth; the latter gives us the satisfaction of recognition. Our reaction to the former may take the form of the question 'Is this what it is like?' to be followed, after a moment's doubt perhaps, by the acceptance, 'This must be what it is like'. Our reaction to the latter is usually 'This is just what it is like' or 'This is just what I have always felt'. In other words, great poetry makes us see something we have never seen before, or have seen but never so clearly; it makes us feel something we have never felt before, or have felt but never so deeply. Few of us, for instance, have had the misfortune to have had our father murdered by our uncle, or to have committed regicide, but Shakespeare makes us feel what it is like to be tormented by the dilemma between intellectual doubts and the desire for revenge, or to be haunted by the remorse and fear of a murderer. Few of us are able to attain to a state of self-oblivious contemplation, but T'ao Ch'ien and Wang Wei enable us, if only momentarily, to be freed from the fetters of our ego and be united with Nature. Or we may have felt the sorrow of separation, but have we ever felt it in the way Li Yü makes us feel it, as a strand of silk:

> Cut it, yet unbroken,
> Arrange it, yet entangled:
> Such is the sorrow of separation?

In short, great poetry either makes us experience new worlds, or makes us experience old worlds in a new way. It can therefore be said that great poetry is not only an expression of reality but an extension of it.

At the same time, since it creates new worlds of experience, great poetry necessarily involves hitherto undiscovered ways of using language, with new expressions, new combinations of

---

[1] It may be recalled that Wang Kuo-wei made the distinction between those who *create* worlds and those who *describe* them, and regarded this as the difference between Idealism and Realism (p. 84). However, as I have observed, all genuine poetry explores a world, not merely describing it. The distinction between those who create new worlds and those who do not, therefore, is not so much one between Idealists and Realists, but one between greater and lesser poets.

sense and sound, new patterns of words, images, symbols, associations. The supreme poet of a language, like Shakespeare or Tu Fu, not only explores more widely and deeply into worlds of human experience but extends the territory of that language more than any other poet. Minor poets may either explore human experience to a greater extent than language, like, say, Wordsworth or Po Chü-I, or do the reverse, like for instance Li Shang-yin or Mallarmé. The relative importance of the two aspects of poetry is a matter for individual taste to decide. All we can say is that without the power of communication in words one may have profound thoughts and noble emotions but still fail as a poet, whereas on the other hand, without great thoughts or deep emotions one can still write good verse inspired by sheer love of words.

To recapitulate: the view of poetry adumbrated above covers elements of various schools of traditional Chinese criticism. In so far as poetry is an exploration of different worlds of experience, it includes self-expression and contemplation, though by no means confined to these. In so far as it is an exploration of language, it is concerned with literary technique. Thus, the Individualist, Intuitional and Technical views, with modifications, can all be reconciled in our view. As for the didactic view, our conception of poetry does not exclude moral, political, or social motives and effects of poetry; it only suggests that these cannot be taken as criteria to judge whether a poem is good or bad. There remains the question how one should write poetry. Since poetry is an exploration of language, every would-be poet should experiment with words, instead of being content with slavish imitation and mechanical application of the rules of versification. Nevertheless, the more he imbues himself with the poetry of the past and the more he studies the art of his predecessors, the more insight will he gain into the behaviour of words and the better will his chances of success be. But what makes one man able to do wonders with words and not another is one of those ultimate mysteries of life which it would be presumptuous for a mere human to enquire into.

2

IMAGERY AND SYMBOLISM

H AVING arrived at our view of poetry as an exploration of
different worlds and of language, we may now turn to
verbal analysis of Chinese poetry, for it is often through such
analysis that we come to perceive what kind of world is being ex-
plored and what new grounds are being broken in the use of
language. In the critical analysis of poetry, imagery and sym-
bolism occupy an important place. But before embarking on any
critical analysis, we have to make clear the meanings of these
terms as used here.

The word 'image' in English is used in various senses, not al-
ways clearly defined. To begin with, there is the iconographic
sense of the word: an image as a physical object. Then there is the
metaphoric sense, as when we speak of 'the very image of truth'.
These two senses are straightforward and need not detain us. But
there are two other senses of the word, which are frequently used
in literary criticism and may cause confusion. On the one hand,
'image' is used to denote a verbal expression that evokes a mental
picture or recalls a physical sensation, not necessarily visual. On
the other hand, the word is used to mean an expression, such as
metaphor, simile, etc., that involves two elements. Indeed, some
writers seem to identify 'image' with 'metaphor'. For instance,
Father S. J. Brown defines imagery as 'words or phrases denoting
a sense-perceptible object, used to designate not that object but
some other object of thought belonging to a different order of
being'.[1] Conversely, Professor I. A. Richards uses 'metaphor' for

[1] *The World of Imagery* (London, 1927), pp. 1–2.

any verbal expression involving two terms (which he calls 'tenor' and 'vehicle'), and seems to extend the range of the word far beyond its normal usage. Thus we are faced with a dilemma of terminology: if we use 'imagery' for both kinds of expressions—those simply recalling physical sensations and those involving two objects—it is likely to lead to confusion; if we use 'metaphor' for the latter, it conflicts with the terminology of traditional rhetoric, for strictly speaking 'metaphor' cannot cover simile, synecdoche, personification, and many other figures of speech also involving two terms, listed by former rhetoricians such as George Puttenham and Abraham Fraunce. To find a way out of this apparent impasse, I propose to distinguish 'simple imagery' from 'compound imagery'. A simple image is a verbal expression that recalls a physical sensation or evokes a mental picture without involving another object; a compound image is one that involves a juxtaposition or a comparison of two objects, or a substitution of one object for another, or a translation of one kind of experience into another. In using the word 'compound', I have in mind a chemical compound consisting of two elements, and do not wish to imply a double-barrelled *form* of expression, as in 'compound sentence'. Once we accept this distinction, we can then avoid the confusion between the two kinds of imagery, and at the same time eschew the use of 'metaphor' beyond its traditional range, for 'compound imagery' can cover other figures of speech which also involve two terms but are formally different from metaphor.

As for 'symbol', it differs from a compound image in several ways. In the first place, a compound image has only a local significance, whereas a symbol is meant to have general significance. 'My love is a red, red rose' constitutes a compound image with a specific reference; the rose as a symbol of Love has universal applicability. This seems to me to be the basic difference between the two, rather than that symbols recur while images do not, as has been suggested.[1] For unless an image is endowed with universal significance, its mere recurrence will not turn it into a symbol. Secondly, a symbol is a physical object chosen to represent something abstract; this is not always the case with a compound image, though some critics seem to think so. We have already seen Father Brown's definition of imagery. A similar statement is John Middleton Murry's assertion that metaphor is

[1] R. Wellek and A. Warren, *Theory of Literature* (New York, 1942), p. 193.

'a definition of indefinable spiritual qualities'.[1] Likewise, Mr. C. Day Lewis also stresses both the sensuous quality of imagery and the spiritual experience it embodies:

> I think that every image—even the most purely emotional or intellectual one—has some trace of the sensuous in it.
>
> . . . the poetic image, as it . . . searches for connections by the light of an impassioned experience, reveals truth and makes it acceptable to us.[2]

But in fact we often encounter compound images involving no spiritual experience but only two physical objects or two kinds of physical experience. For instance, in 'Sleep, . . . great Nature's second course', two kinds of physical experience are involved. In

> Thou art fairer than the evening's air,
> Clad in the beauty of a thousand stars,

only physical objects are involved in the compound image: Helen is compared to the evening air lit by the stars. Someone might argue that emotion is involved here, not merely physical sensations. To which I would reply: of course I do not deny that emotion is being expressed by the image, but my point is that the whole compound image, with its tenor (Helen) and vehicle (star-clad air), bodies forth the emotion, while the two terms themselves consist of physical objects only. It is only in images like

> The wine of life is drawn, and the mere lees
> Is left this vault to brag of

that we see spiritual experience described in terms of physical experience. Moreover, sometimes we even find the reverse: imagery describing physical experience in terms of mental experience, such as

> With wings as swift as *meditation* or the *thought* of love

or

> Darker grows the valley, more and more *forgetting*.

In short, a compound image need not involve more than physical experience, while a symbol is a physical object representing a

---

[1] *Countries of the Mind*, 2nd series (London, 1931), p. 9.
[2] *The Poetic Image* (London, 1947), pp. 19 and 34.

spiritual experience or an abstract idea. Another difference between compound imagery and symbols is that with a compound image we can usually tell what are the two terms concerned, though it may be difficult to say which is the tenor and which the vehicle,[1] or to name the vehicle while having no difficulty in identifying the tenor;[2] but with a symbol, especially a personal one, it is often difficult to identify the tenor (what is represented), though the vehicle (thing chosen to represent something else) is always named. We all recognize 'Tiger, tiger, burning bright' as a symbol, but what does it symbolize? One might say that it symbolizes energy or creative imagination, but it would be an over-simplification. That is why, it seems to me, the tiger in Blake's poem is a symbol and not just a compound image.

Of course, the boundary line between imagery and symbolism is not a hard and fast one. A compound image, or even a simple one, while serving the immediate purpose of describing a person or an object, may at the same time be endowed with wider significance and thus become symbolic as well. My purpose in drawing the above distinctions is not to establish rigid categories but to clarify the different processes by which different kinds of verbal expressions produce their effect in poetry.

Let us now consider the use of imagery and symbolism in Chinese poetry. We shall begin with simple imagery. Naturally, we find numerous simple images in Chinese poetry, as in any other poetry, for it is the nature of poetic language to be concrete rather than abstract. Moreover, as I pointed out in Part I, the language of Chinese poetry is extremely concise and often dispenses with connecting particles,[3] so that a line can consist of a sequence of images. Such images are not merely pictures in words: they arouse emotional associations and enrich their poetic context. For example, in the poem 'The Gentle Maiden' quoted on p. 23, there are several simple images: a tower, a red pipe, the pasture, and a shoot. I will try to demonstrate what emotional associations are evoked by these images, but in order to do so it is necessary to consider the meaning of the whole poem. This will incidentally also explain why I translated certain words in the way I did. To save the reader the trouble of going back and forth, I will repeat my translation of the poem here:

[1] See William Empson, *The Structure of Complex Words*, pp. 345–6.
[2] See below, p. 109.   [3] See above, p. 41.

How pretty is the gentle maiden!
At the tower of the city wall she should be waiting.
I love her but I cannot see her;
I scratch my head while anxiously pacing.

The gentle maiden: how lovely is she!
This red pipe she gave to me.
O red pipe, with lustre bright,
Your beauty gives me great delight.

From the pasture she sent me her plight—
A tender shoot, beautiful and rare.
Yet it's not your beauty that gives me delight,
But she who sent you, so true and fair!

Like other poems in *The Book of Poetry*, this simple love song
has been extensively annotated by generations of commentators
and sub-commentators, some of whom would have us believe
that this is a satire on a certain ancient queen who was not gentle
and modest as the girl in the poem. To me this is too far-fetched;
and I prefer to take the poem as a simple love song, describing a
young man's anxiety while waiting for his beloved, and his re-
assurance as he looks at the love-tokens she has sent him and
meditates on her beauty. In the first line, the character *ching* 靜,
usually meaning 'quiet', here implies a gentle and modest dis-
position. Some commentators have doubted the appropriateness
of this epithet for a girl who goes to a secret tryst and therefore
labelled this poem a 'lewd song', but these pedants forgot that
even if the girl's conduct should be regarded as immodest, it
would not appear so to her lover! In the second line, the character
yü 隅 has the usual meaning 'corner', but I have adopted the
interpretation of the late Wen I-to that here it refers to the tower
at the corner of the city wall, as it seems more sensible to arrange
a rendezvous in the tower rather than simply at the corner of the
wall. In the next line, the character *ai* 愛 ('love') has a homo-
phonous variant reading *ai* 薆 ('obscure'), and the whole line has
been taken by Dr. Arthur Waley to mean, 'She hides herself and
will not let me see her.' I prefer, however, the more straight-
forward interpretation 'I love her but cannot see her.' In the
second stanza, the red pipe has been a subject of much learned
discussion. It may be a musical instrument or a writing brush.
The former seems to me more satisfying from the aesthetic point
of view, and also has more relevant associations, as I will describe

below. In stanza 2, line 4, the character *nü* 女 ('girl') could be taken as being a loan for *ju* 汝 ('you'). If one chooses the former sense, the line then means, 'I delight in the beauty of the girl'. But I think it is better to choose the latter sense, 'you', and take the line as addressed to the pipe: 'I delight in your (i.e. pipe's) beauty', for this is paralleled by the last two lines of the final stanza, where the same character is taken by all scholars to mean 'you', not 'girl'. In identifying *nü* with *ju* in the second stanza, I have the authority of the Ch'ing scholars Yao Chi-heng (born 1647) and Wang Hsien-ch'ien (1842–1918) as well as the contemporary scholar Professor Yü P'ing-po.

So much for the meaning of the poem. Let us now return to the imagery. The images in his poem, though few, are fresh and lively, and arouse emotional associations in keeping with the mood. The tower suggests intimacy and secrecy; the pipe suggests music and gaiety; the pasture suggests the freedom of outdoor life; and the young shoot, tender and white, reminds one of the girl's fair skin (the same image is in fact used in another song in the same anthology to describe a woman's hands), and may further suggest youth and purity. They thus all help to convey the lover's tender feelings for the girl and his appreciation of her beauty. These images are delicate and natural, just as the emotion they help to express is delicate rather than passionate. We may notice the contrast in colour between the red pipe and the white shoot, though they are similar in shape. The similarity between these images strengthens the structure of the poem, which is built on reiteration and parallelism. The lover first looks at the pipe, then at the shoot, both being presents from his beloved, and admires their beauty; only at the end of the poem does he directly express his feeling for the girl herself, thus reaching an emotional climax as the poem closes.

As for compound imagery, we may distinguish several types, not according to formal distinctions such as those between simile and metaphor, but according to different degrees of connection between the two objects involved in the image. First of all, there are compound images which simply put two objects side by side without making any overt or covert comparison between them; then there are those which liken one thing to another; then those which describe one thing as if it were another; finally those which attribute to an object qualities not normally attributable to it.

These images differ from one another in degree rather than in kind: they represent various stages of the same mental process— that of connecting two things. We may designate these stages juxtaposition, comparison, substitution, and transference, respectively.

Compound images involving juxtaposition often appear at first sight to be only simple ones, as they do not compare one thing to another but simply put a natural phenomenon side by side with a human situation, so as to suggest an analogy or a contrast. Such images are very common in Chinese poetry. For instance, in *The Book of Poetry*, there is an epithalamium that begins:

> The peach-tree is young and tender:
> Bright, bright, its blossoms shine.
> This young lady is getting married:
> May she become her house and home!

The poet does not compare the young bride to the peach-tree, but few readers will miss the suggested analogy between the two. At the same time, the peach-tree with its blossoms can also be regarded as a simple image describing the season. Such imagery, therefore, often has a dual function—describing an immediate object and pointing at an analogy or contrast at the same time.

Sometimes it is difficult to say whether a poet intended his images to be simple ones, for descriptive purposes only, or meant them to be compound ones as well. However that may be, we can regard images as compound ones if by so doing we can gain a better understanding of the poem, whether they are consciously intended to be such or not. For example, in the following poem by Tu Fu entitled 'Thinking of Li Po On a Spring Day', we find two simple images that can be taken as compound ones at the same time:

> O Po, whose poetry none can emulate,
> Whose thoughts soar above the common crowd!
> Pure and fresh like the verse of Minister Yü;
> Graceful and free like that of Counsellor Pao.
> The spring trees north of the river Wei,
> The evening clouds east of the Great River.
> When will we, over a jug of wine,
> Discuss in detail the art of writing again?

After eulogizing Li Po and comparing his poetry to that of two earlier poets, Yü Hsin and Pao Chao, Tu Fu introduces the two images—spring trees and evening clouds—that have no apparent connection with the preceding lines. Of course, their immediate purpose is to describe the two places where Tu Fu and Li Po happen to be: while the one is looking at the trees north of the river Wei, the other is roaming under the clouds east of the Great River (i.e. the Yangtze). But it is possible that the two images were suggested to Tu Fu, through conscious or unconscious association, by the two pairs of adjectives he had used in the previous couplet: 'pure and fresh', and 'graceful and free'. The images give body to these epithets and thus become compound images comparing qualities of Li Po's poetry to the spring trees and evening clouds. In this way the apparent break in the middle of the poem is bridged and the structure of the whole tightened.

Images involving comparison of one thing to another also occur often in Chinese poetry. The comparison may be explicitly stated, such as in

> Bright as the moon is she who serves the wine,

or in

> Over the river the willows are thick as mist,

or implied, such as in

> The perfumed candle has dissolved in tears.

In fact, Chinese poetry is riddled with hackneyed images like 'cloudy hair', 'starry eyes', 'flowery face', etc. I will discuss later what critical attitude we should adopt towards such images.

Images involving substitution differ from the above type in that the tenor is not mentioned but simply substituted by the vehicle. For instance, instead of saying 'starry eyes' one simply says 'stars' for 'eyes'. Again, we encounter many *clichés* among images of this kind, such as 'autumn waves' for 'eyes', 'emerald strips' for 'willow twigs', etc.

Of particular interest are images that substitute one kind of sensation for another, such as 'bitter rain'. Such images of course occur in daily speech, both in Chinese and in English, as when one speaks of a 'loud tie'. Some writers call this kind of compound imagery 'synaesthetic metaphors', but strictly speaking this is not an accurate term, for such images do not *combine* several senses but substitute one sense for another. They should therefore be called, if anything, 'transaesthetic images'. However, genuine synaesthetic images do exist in Chinese poetry. For instance, the moon-light is often compared to snow, frost, or water. In each case two senses are involved: visual and thermal, for all these images suggest not only whiteness but coolness. To take another example, the young lover in the *Romance of the Western Chamber* describes his lady as 'soft jade and warm perfume'—two images combining several senses that effectively express his passion. As a contrast, we may look at another example of synaesthetic imagery. This time a lady is described as having 'ice flesh and jade bones'. Here the suggestion of coolness creates a distance between the lady and us, as if she were no common mortal but an object of aesthetic contemplation. This is as it should be: the lady in question is the favourite of Meng Ch'ang, King of Shu, who wrote the poem containing this phrase and who may well have intended this 'cooling effect' in an otherwise somewhat erotic poem.

Next we come to images that attribute to objects qualities or actions not normally attributable to them. For instance, in a poem on the moon, Tu Fu begins with the line

> At the fourth watch,[1] the mountains exhale a moon.

The word I have translated as 'exhale', *t'u*,[2] usually means 'to eject from the mouth', but unfortunately there does not seem to be any English word that means exactly the same without un-pleasant associations. Anyway, it is easy to see the use of this verb constitutes a compound image, but it is hard to name the vehicle of the image: to what are the mountains compared? We can, of course, say that they are compared to animals, or human beings, or one huge mouth perhaps, but if we try to visualize the moun-tains as any of these, it will spoil the effect of the image. The poet's intention is not to liken the mountains to anything definite, but simply to suggest the gradual emergence of the moon as if ejected by the enclosing mountains. There is no need, therefore, to identify the vehicle of the compound image, which involves a transference of an attribute from objects not specified to an object to which it does not normally belong, but does not involve a com-parison of one object to another.

[1] The night used to be divided into five watches, the fourth watch corre-sponding roughly to 1 to 3 a.m.

[2] The word is pronounced here in the Rising Tone. When pronounced in the Falling Tone it means 'vomit'. Only then does it have unpleasant associa-tions.

For the sake of clarity I have treated the various kinds of imagery separately. In actual fact, however, they naturally occur together sometimes, and indeed, as I have already shown, some images can act as both simple and compound images simultaneously. Let us now examine a poem in which several types of imagery are used. It is a lyric to the tune *P'u-sa Man* by Wen T'ing-yun:

> The manifold hills look golden and dark upon the panelled screen,
> Her cloudy hair droops over the snow of her fragrant cheeks.
> Too lazy to rise and paint her eyebrows,
> Over her make-up she dallies and delays.
>
> Mirrors before and behind reflect a flower;
> The flower and her face on each other shine.
> Her newly made silk jacket is embroidered
> With golden partridges flying two by two.

To anyone unfamiliar with this kind of Chinese poetry, this poem may seem just a pretty picture of a pretty girl. It is in fact more than that. In the first line, the hills refer to the scenery painted or carved on a bedside screen consisting of several panels and usually arranged in a zigzag fashion. Hence, the hills are 'manifold' not only because they are painted so but also because they are on a manifold screen: and since half of the panels face the light and the other half are in the shade, they create a chiaroscuro effect and make the hills look alternately 'golden and dark'. The word 'golden' could refer to the sunshine, or to the gold decorating the screen, or to both. In any case, whether we take it as a simple image describing the golden decorations or a compound image comparing the sunshine to gold, together with the hills it gives a vivid picture of a boudoir scene set in a rich, cultured, and leisured *milieu*. Moreover, the image of Nature in the first line leads easily to the compound images in the next line: the *cloud* of her hair and the *snow* of her cheeks. By using images drawn from Nature in both lines, the poet has imperceptibly blended the actual world with the imaginary: the hills on the screen, the sunshine, the imagined cloud and snow, all merge into one another to form a homogeneous world of its own. In the second stanza, images of juxtaposition are used. The flower is intended as an analogy to the girl, while the embroidered pairs of golden partridges call attention to a contrast. The girl is looking into a mirror in front, while holding another mirror behind her head, as she tries to put a flower on her hair. The delicate beauty of the flower gives her a wistful feeling and reminds her of the fragile nature of her own beauty and youth, while the happy pairs of birds embroidered on her jacket form an ironic contrast to her solitary state. The whole poem is seen to be not merely a portrait of a pretty girl but an expression of a young girl's half-understood, first awakening to love. It somehow reminds one of Meredith's *Love in the Valley*:

> She knows not why, but now she loiters,
> Eyes the bent anemones, and hangs her hands.
> Such a look will tell that the violets are peeping,
> Coming the rose; and unaware a cry
> Springs in her bosom for odours and for colour,
> Covert and the nightingale, she knows not why.

Sometimes imagery can be used together with puns. In the line I quoted once before (p. 11):

> The sun comes out in the east, it rains in the west;
> You'll say it's not sunny (love), yet it is,

the pun on 'sunny' and 'love', both pronounced *ch'ing*, can be regarded at the same time as a compound image: fickle love is compared to fitful sunshine. To take another example, the poet Han Hung had a concubine surnamed Liu ('willow'). When he left the capital to take up an official post elsewhere, he left her behind, and she was subsequently abducted by a general of foreign origin. In his dismay Han Hung sent her this poem:

> Willow of Chang Terrace,
> Willow of Chang Terrace!
> Is the fresh green of former days still there?
> No, even if the long branches are drooping as before,
> Someone else's hand must have plucked them now!

To which she replied:

> Willow, willow branch,
> During the season of flowers:
> Why must it be made a parting present every year?
> A leaf, following the wind, suddenly heralds the coming of
> autumn;
> Even if you come again, how can it be worth plucking
> still?

In both poems, 'willow' is used as a compound image as well as a pun on the woman's name. By likening her to a helpless, fragile willow, the image brings out the pathos of her situation and saves the pun from being a mere frivolous play on words. It should be further pointed out that Chang Terrace is a euphemism for a house of courtesans, and that, as I mentioned once before (p. 11), it was a custom to present a willow twig to a departing friend (hence the third line in the second poem). Such implications and associations further emphasize her pathetic, defenceless position—a wayside willow to be plucked and cherished if it took the fancy of a passer-by, or left to be ravaged by the rough weather.

The same image-cum-pun is used by Li Shang-yin in a number of his poems. In some of these, as he himself made clear in notes, 'willow' refers to a young girl called 'Willow Branch', who admired the poet but whose love he missed through accidental circumstances. In others it seems to be a veiled reference to one of his patrons, surnamed Liu ('willow').

Such punning images add a pungent flavour to the verse, and can also stress the particular appropriateness of an image (as when the word forming the image puns on the name of the person to whom it is applied). They are comparable to, though usually less elaborate than, Shakespeare's famous puns on 'hart' and 'heart', etc. Apart from puns, imagery can of course also be combined with other auditory devices, such as onomatopoeia. I have already given an example of onomatopoeic imagery on p. 37, and no more examples are necessary here.

So far I have discussed imagery in Chinese poetry as a whole, drawing examples from various periods of poetry without discrimination. But in fact, if we compare earlier Chinese poetry with later poetry, especially if we compare the poetry before Tu Fu with his poetry and that of many poets after him, we will see considerable differences in the use of imagery. In the first place, in earlier poetry simple imagery and compound imagery involving only juxtaposition occur frequently, while compound imagery involving comparison, substitution, and transference is used less. In later poetry, all types of imagery are used, without marked predominance of any one type. Secondly, in earlier poetry the use of imagery tends to be casual and simple, while in later poetry it is often deliberate and complicated. Furthermore, in earlier poetry we seldom find the same image used throughout a poem, or different images closely connected with one another by associations, while in later poetry we encounter sustained imagery and underlying unity of imagery.

Imagery and Symbolism

The following poem by Juan Chi (210–263), one in a series entitled 'Expressing his Thoughts', may be given as an example of earlier poetry:

> It is midnight, yet I cannot sleep,
> So I sit up to play upon my strings.
> The thin curtain reveals a brilliant moon,
> The cool wind my dress gently swings.
> Out in the wild a single swan cries,
> In the northern wood a flying bird sings.
> Pacing to and fro, what can I see?
> A sorrowful thought my lonely heart wrings.

The use of imagery here is natural and simple. The moon and the wind are simple images which do not appear to be intended for any purpose other than that of description. The wild swan and the singing bird may be taken as compound images drawing an analogy between these birds crying unhappily at night and the poet singing alone in a world full of darkness. It has been suggested that the wild swan represents a virtuous official away from Court, while the flying bird represents a vicious official in power. This seems to me pedantic and unnecessary. Be that as it may, the imagery consists of analogies that might easily strike anyone in such a situation, not far-fetched and elaborately developed comparisons like those we find in some later poems. Also, the various images occur together because the objects involved happen to be present at the same time, not because there is any particular underlying relation among them, as is sometimes the case with later poetry.

Let us now turn to a later poem which pursues a single analogy throughout the poem:

To a Friend, in Jest

> If for one day I do not write poetry,
> My mind's source dries as a deserted well.
> The brush and ink-slab are my pulleys,
> Humming and chanting are my winding ropes.
> Next morning I pull and draw again,
> Once more I get a clear draught.
> —I write this for a like-minded man:
> Our verses are full of hardships and bitterness!

Here, the poet, Chia Tao (777–841), deliberately develops the analogy between writing poetry and drawing water from a well in great detail, in a manner that recalls the Metaphysical Poets.

As a matter of fact, some later Chinese poets resemble the Metaphysical Poets also in their use of far-fetched conceits, while earlier poets are generally content with comparisons that may easily occur to anyone. Take for example the following images used by Han Yü (768–824): the sun and moon are compared to two balls thrown alternately into the air; those who belittle the poetry of Li Po and Tu Fu are described as 'ants trying to shake a big tree'; and the sound of falling leaves in autumn makes the poet suspect that Wang Shu, the Driver of the Moon Chariot, had fallen with his orb—a conceit that reminds one of Phaeton and his fall. Or take this Quatrain by Han Yü's friend Meng Chiao (751–814), a poem put in the mouth of a woman:

> Let us, you and me, drop our tears
> Into our separate ponds, there and here;
> And then take the lotus-flowers to see
> For which of us they have died this year.

Apart from conceiving original and striking imagery, later poets also prefer to use images related to each other through common associations. In the two lyrics by Wen T'ing-yan given on p. 58, the poet twice uses the images of incense burning to ashes and candle melting in tears. It is easy to see why these two images are used together: both suggest a self-consuming passion and both are associated with intimate indoor scenes and therefore evoke the same kind of atmosphere.

The above differences in the use of imagery between earlier and later poets lead us to a consideration of the problem of what criteria to adopt for imagery in Chinese poetry. We cannot judge imagery purely by the criterion of originality, for in a language with such a long history as Chinese it is clearly impossible to use original imagery all the time. The question, then, is: how are we to judge whether an image in a given poem is good or bad apart from the question of its being original or otherwise? I propose the following points for consideration.

First, we should remember that hackneyed images must have been original once, and before condemning a poem as full of hackneyed images we should first ask when it was written—in other words, whether the images were already hackneyed when the poet used them. It would be as absurd to say that *The Book of*

Poetry and *The Songs of Ch'u* are full of hackneyed imagery as to say that Shakespeare is full of quotations. Naturally it will require some effort to restore to an image that has become a *cliché* its original force, but this is the only way to be fair to the poet who first conceived it. The problem is further complicated when we think of Chinese poetry in translation. Ironically, a hackneyed image may not appear as such in translation; on the contrary, it may seem quite original and striking to the reader who does not know the original language. 'Autumn waves', a *cliché* in Chinese for a woman's eyes, appears almost daring, if a little quaint, in English, as it must have done in Chinese when first used in *The Songs of Ch'u*. We are thus faced with a dilemma: whether to point out hackneyed imagery as such, or to give it a false aura of originality in translation. Personally I believe that though as a translator one might secretly congratulate oneself on the lucky chance of restoring to a *cliché* some of its original force and splendour, as a critic and interpreter of Chinese poetry to Western readers one should not hesitate to point out hackneyed images in any critical analysis or evaluation of a poem.

Next we should ask how the image is used: what poetic purpose it serves, irrespective of whether it is original or not. The effect of imagery does not depend entirely on its originality; for whereas an original image can stimulate the imagination of the reader by its novelty, a conventional one can, by its very familiarity, more readily call forth the desired response and the relevant associations. If the poet uses images which have similar associations to build up a coherent picture, or if he uses a conventional image but gives it a twist or a fresh significance in a new context, or if he further develops such an image or modifies it to suit his present purpose, then it matters little whether the imagery is original or not. We have already seen several poems in which images with similar associations are used to build up a homogeneous picture and produce a unified effect (the poems quoted on pp. 51, 56, 58, 105). We can now look at some examples of the various means by which poets strove to avoid *clichés* while borrowing imagery from other poets.

First of all, a poet can use a conventional compound image but develop the comparison further, or add subtle variations to the central analogy. The following poem by Wang An-shih (1021–1086) is a good example.

Towards a Synthesis

Almond Blossoms

A stone bridge spans the vast void,
A thatched hut overlooks the clear water.
Bending to peep at the delicate almond blooms,
I feel the image is as good as the original:
Charming as the Lady of the Ching-yang Palace
Who, smiling, leapt into the well.
Sad it is to see the tiny ripples
Spoil her fading make-up beyond repair.

It is quite common to compare a beautiful lady to flowers and *vice versa*, but Wang An-shih has developed this conventional comparison in several interesting ways. First, instead of likening the almond blossoms themselves to a beautiful lady, he compares the reflected image of the blossoms in water to a lady who drowned herself, so that the comparison at once ceases to be hackneyed and perfunctory but becomes specific and apt. (The Lady of the Ching-yang Palace refers to a favourite of the last ruler of the Ch'en dynasty.) Next, the poet works out further details of analogy between the reflection of the blossoms and the lady throwing herself into the well: both are charming in spite of their fragile nature, and both have their beauty spoiled by the ripples on the water. The identification of the two is suggested by the use of the deliberately ambiguous word 'original' (literally, 'body') in the fourth line, and becomes complete in the last line, where the broken reflection of the blossoms and the spoilt make-up of the drowned beauty are one and the same.

Next, a borrowed image can be given a twist in a new context. For instance, the Sung poet Su Shih, better known as Su Tung-po (1036–1101), used two images to describe wine:

It should be called 'the hook that fishes poetry',
Also termed 'the broomstick that sweeps away sorrow'.

These images are borrowed by the Yuan dramatic poet Ch'iao Chi (?–1345) in his play *The Golden Coins* (*Chin-ch'ien Chi*), in which a lovesick young man refuses to be consoled by wine:

This 'sorrow-sweeping broomstick' cannot sweep away my
  melancholy;
This 'poetry-fishing hook' cannot fish my lovesickness.

Thus, the original comparisons are kept but the ideas behind them are turned upside down.

Sometimes, one can modify a borrowed image and derive a slightly different one from it. In the same play the young man tries to imagine his beloved lying in bed:

> Her thick coverlet folds its *red clouds*.

This image is a modified version of the poetess Li Ch'ing-chao's original one:

> The coverlet turns its *red waves*.

Furthermore, one can use two conventional images in antithesis so as to give them some fresh force. In the play *Over the Wall and On the Horse* (*Ch'iang-t'ou Ma-shang*), a romantic comedy by Pai P'u (1226–cir. 1313), the dramatic poet uses the following imagery:

> The shady willows form a thick green mist,
> The fading flowers fly in red showers.

Neither of these images is original, but when put in a meticulous antithetical couplet as they are here, they acquire fresh force which each by itself would no longer possess.

In addition to the above ways of using borrowed imagery, which can be used in all kinds of poetry, there are others in which a dramatic poet in particular can use imagery for dramatic purposes.

The use to which imagery is most frequently put in Chinese dramatic poetry is describing scenery, thereby helping the audience to visualize the physical background of the action and creating an appropriate atmosphere. Examples can be found in any poetic drama. The following passage, describing a moonlit garden in spring where a young lady and her maid are taking a stroll, is from *The Sophisticated Maid* (*Chou Mei-hsiang*) by Cheng Kuang-tzu (early fourteenth century):

> The wind stirring the cherry-apple blossoms: a loom weaving a piece of cold 'mermaid silk';
> The mist on the fragrant grass: a verdurous gauze over clear glass;
> The dew drops on the drooping willows: pearls strung with green silk threads;
> The stars reflected in the pond: scattered crystal balls on a jade plate;
> The moon above the top of the pine-tree: an ancient mirror held by a grey dragon.

By means of these eleborate images, the dramatic poet conjures up a beautiful scene, thus providing a suitable atmosphere for the ensuing action: the young lady overhears a scholar playing his zither, which of course marks the beginning of a love story.

To move on to a totally different world, we may turn to *Rain on the Wu-t'ung Trees*, which deals with the well-known story of the Emperor Ming Huang of the T'ang dynasty and his favourite Yang Kuei-fei, and from which an example of onomatopoeic imagery has been given on p. 37 in the present volume. The scene is the palace, and the Emperor is sitting up late at night in sorrow after the death of his favourite. He hears the rain beating on the *wu-t'ung* trees—the same trees under which he has stood with her and sworn eternal love to her. Here are some of the images describing the rain:

> Now it is fast,
> Like ten thousand pearls dropping on a jade plate;
> Then it is loud,
> Like several groups of musicians and singers at a banquet;
> Now it is clear,
> Like a cold cataract falling on mossy rocks;
> Again it becomes fierce,
> Like some battle drums booming under embroidered banners.

Images like the above ones can evoke the right kind of atmosphere for the action and put the audience in a sympathetic mood. Their effect is comparable to those produced by scenery and stage lighting in the modern theatre. Of course, such use of imagery in poetic drama is also found in other languages. To take one or two examples at random, at the opening of *Agamemnon*, Aeschylus uses imagery to produce an atmosphere of darkness and forlorn hope:

> Twelve full months now, night after night
> Dog-like I lie here, keeping guard from this high roof
> On Atreus' palace. The nightly conference of stars,
> Resplendent rulers, bringing heat and cold in turn,
> Studding the sky with beauty—I know them all, and watch them
> Setting and rising.[1]

Similarly, in *Doctor Faustus*, Marlowe uses imagery of darkness to provide a suitable setting for Faustus to practise black magic:

[1] Translated by Philip Vellacott (Penguin Classics), p. 41.

Now that the gloomy shadow of the night
Longing to view Orion's drizzling look,
Leaps from th'antarctic world unto the sky,
And dims the welkin with her pitchy breath,
Faustus, begin thine incantations,
And try if devils will obey thy hest.
                    (Act I, sc. iii)

Apart from describing scenery, imagery can be used to express the emotions of the characters in a play. As a matter of fact, imagery is used as a means of expressing emotion in all kinds of poetry; only, in dramatic poetry it is the emotion of the characters and not of the author himself that is bodied forth by imagery. A few examples will suffice to show how Chinese dramatic poets used imagery for such a purpose. In the tragedy *Autumn in the Han Palace (Han Kung Ch'iu)* by Ma Chih-yuan (cir. 1270–1330), the Emperor of Han, while bidding farewell to his favourite Wang Chao-chün, who is being forced to go to Mongolia and marry the Khan as a means of appeasement, expresses his grief by these images:

> Brief as the golden bridle is our former love,
> Long as the jade-handled whip our present sorrow.

In this way, their former love and present plight are brought into sharp contrast. Moreover, since the speaker is supposed to be on horse-back, these images do not strike one as far-fetched but natural and apt.

Another example may be given from a comedy, *The Gold-thread Pond (Chin-hsien Ch'ih)* by Kuan Han-ch'ing (thirteenth century). The speaker is a courtesan who thinks her lover has deserted her:

The Eastern Ocean could not wash away the shame on my face;
The West Hua Mountain could not conceal the disgrace of my person;
A demon of great strength could not unlock my knitted eyebrows;
No mighty river god could break the sorrow in my breast.

These images are fantastic and somewhat absurd, but it seems the author is purposely exaggerating so as to produce a comic effect, for we know that the lover has not really deserted her and that there is no occasion for such excessive grief. Incidentally, the first image in this passage naturally reminds one of Macbeth's famous cry,

> Will all great Neptune's ocean wash this blood
> Clean from my hand?

And Shakespeare, as has been pointed out,[1] may have derived his image from Seneca's *Hippolytus*:

> *non ipse toto magnus Oceano pater tantum expiarit sceleris.*

Such coincidences illustrate how minds widely separated in space and time can conceive similar imagery.

Sometimes the two purposes of imagery in dramatic poetry mentioned above—describing scenery and expressing the emotions of the characters—are combined. A perfect example occurs in the famous parting scene of the *Romance of the Western Chamber*. The hero and heroine are forced to part from one another after a brief happy union, and the heroine opens the scene thus:

> Grey clouds in the sky,
> Yellow flowers on the ground,
> The west wind blowing hard,
> The wild geese southward flying.
> In the early morning who has dyed the frosty trees with drunken hue?
> Ah, it must be parting lovers' tears!

Here we have a wonderful mixed metaphor: first the frosty leaves are described as having been 'dyed' red; then they are likened to the flushed faces of drunken people; finally they are said to have been turned red by parting lovers' tears. Thus we get at once a vivid picture of an autumn wood and an effective expression of the lovers' sorrow, for the conceit that their tears have turned the leaves red suggest that they are shedding blood from their eyes.

In another play, *The Girl Whose Soul Left Her Body (Ch'ien-nü Li-hun)* by Cheng Kuang-tzu, the heroine, pining away when separated from her fiancé, shows her feelings in these images:

> Long is the day, but my sorrow longer;
> Scarce are the red flowers, scarcer his letters.

These images also combine the functions of description of scenery and expression of emotion: they reveal her ennui and solitude while simultaneously indicating the season—end of spring and beginning of summer, when the day is growing longer and the flowers are fading away.

The above examples illustrate how imagery can fulfil a dual purpose in dramatic poetry. In fact, the examples given earlier from Aeschylus and Marlowe can also be shown to fulfil this dual

---

[1] *Notes and Queries*, Vol. 196, p. 337.

purpose: in the passage from *Agamemnon*, the images of dark night and stars not only describe the scene of the action but reveal the prevailing mood of weariness and foreboding among the citizens of Argos (as suggested by the night) and their hope for the coming of light (as suggested by the stars); in the passage from *Faustus*, the imagery shows the hero's state of mind in addition to creating an atmosphere of darkness: just as the gloomy shadow of the night, impatient to see the storm presaged by Orion, spreads over the sky, so does the power of evil, eager to see the destruction of Faustus's soul, exert its influence over his mind.

Another dramatic purpose imagery can fulfil is to describe a character and influence our attitude towards him or her. In Ma Chih-yuan's *Tears on the Dark Gown* (*Ch'ing-shan Lei*), which deals with the alleged love between the poet Po Chü-I and the singing girl P'ei Hsing-nu, the latter complains of her fate thus:

> The fallen leaf is like my person that has to answer the biddings of officials.

As a 'public courtesan' (*kuan chi*) she has to appear at official banquets to entertain the guests when summoned to do so. This pathetic fate is underlined by the image of the fallen leaf, which induces our sympathy for her. In similar fashion, another singing girl, in the play named after her, *Hsieh T'ien-hsiang* by Kuan Han-ch'ing, compares herself to a caged bird:

> You say the parrot in the golden cage can recite verse;
> This is a fit comparison for me:
> The cleverer one is, the harder to get out of the cage.

The above two images somewhat resemble two images used by Shakespeare and Marlowe to describe, respectively, Macbeth in his last hour and Edward II in captivity:

> My way of life
> Is fall'n to the sear, the yellow leaf.
> (*Macbeth*, Act V, scene iii)

> The wren may strive against the lion's strength,
> But all in vain: so vainly do I strive
> To seek for mercy at a tyrant's hand.
> (*Edward II*, Act V, scene iii)

Different as the dramatic situations are, imagery in each case sums up a character in a given situation and influences our emotional attitude towards him or her.

The dramatic effects of imagery can be enhanced by recurrence. Although recurrent imagery of the Shakespearean kind, which forms an underlying pattern throughout the play, is not found in Chinese poetic drama, we do occasionally encounter images that recur a few times in a play. For instance, in the *Romance of the Western Chamber*, the image of tears of blood that turned the leaves red mentioned above is followed up later when the heroine says:

> The front and sleeves of my dress are wet with red tears,

and again:

> Blood flows from my eyes while my heart turns to ashes.

Another recurrent image is found in *Rain on the Wu-t'ung Trees*. When the Imperial Guards refuse to escort the Emperor unless his favourite Yang Kuei-fei is killed, he pleads with them:

> She is a delicate cherry-apple blossom;
> How could she be the root of troubles that would ruin the
>   country?

In the final scene, he recalls her death:

> Alas, that the cherry-apple blossom should have withered!

Because of this recurrent image, the cherry-apple blossom becomes associated in our mind with Yang Kuei-fei: we think of her as this flower—her beauty just as delicate and her life as brief.

In short, in Chinese poetry, especially in dramatic poetry, one can often borrow imagery from others, but, by using various means, endow such imagery with fresh force and significance so as to redeem it from its hackneyed state.

A different problem to that of hackneyed images is presented by expressions which were originally conceived as compound images but which have long since ceased to be so used. Such expressions in English are commonly called 'dead' or 'fossilized' metaphors. It may be, as Professor I. A. Richards said, that all language is ultimately metaphorical, but for purposes of practical criticism we have to draw the line somewhere between what is intended to be metaphorical and what is not. Our problem is where to draw the line. While it is impossible to lay down hard and fast rules, it is generally possible to judge by the context whether a metaphor (or compound image, to revert to my own terminology) is intended. For instance, it is safe to assume that in speaking of 'investing money' most people do not have the image of clothes in mind. The same is true of similar expressions in Chinese. As I pointed out in Part I, Chapter 2, many of the original metaphorical implications of Chinese characters have long been lost, and if we were to insist on treating every character as a metaphor, we would lapse into the same errors made by Fenollosa, Pound, and others. On the whole, we may assume a word or phrase to be not metaphorical unless there are indications to the contrary. In a lyric to the tune *P'u-sa Man*, attributed to Li Po and often cited as the earliest known specimen of poetry in Lyric Metres, the opening lines run as follows:

> The woods upon the plain are woven with a thick mist,
> The chilly mountains lie, a belt of melancholy green.

What I have translated as 'a belt', *yi tai* 一 帶, could mean simply 'a stretch', or 'a region', without metaphorical implications. However, I think in the present context I am justified in taking the expression in its original sense, as the poet has used the word 'woven' in the preceding line, and it is probable that he had in mind the picture of a green belt lying against a background of grey woven fabric, to which the mist is compared. In contrast to this example, when Tu Fu wrote the line

> Over the windy woods a slender moon sets,

in all probability he did not intend the word *hsien* ('slender') to be metaphorical, though the character for this word, 纖, contains the 'silk' significant. It was pure fancy on the part of Florence Ayscough to suggest that the poet intended to describe a pattern like that of woven silk, as the adjective is applied to the moon itself, not to the shadow it casts.[1]

There remains one more point about imagery to be considered: imagery as a revelation of the poet's personality. Since 'style is the man himself', imagery, which plays an important part in forming one's style, often provides a clue to the man. By a happy coincidence, we have three very similar couplets written by the three greatest poets of the T'ang dynasty, Wang Wei, Li Po, and Tu Fu

[1] See William Hung, *Tu Fu*, pp. 10–11.

(in the order of their births). The couplets in question are as follows:

> The river's flow (lies) beyond heaven and earth,
> The mountain's colour between being and non-being.
> > —Wang Wei, 'Sailing on the Han River'

> The mountains, following the wild plain, come to an end;
> The river, entering the great waste, flows.
> > —Li Po, 'Crossing the Chingmen Mountain to See a Friend Off'

> The stars drooping, the wild plain (is) vast;
> The moon rushing, the great river flows.
> > —Tu Fu, 'Expressing his Thoughts While Travelling at Night.'

All three poems describe a river scene in what is now Hupeh province, but each reveals a different world and a different personality through the imagery. Wang Wei, by using the abstract 'flow' and 'colour' instead of the concrete 'river' and 'mountain' as subjects, and by describing these as lying beyond heaven and earth and between being and non-being, creates a sense of other-worldliness that makes the whole scene appear illusory. This is an expression, conscious or not, of the poet's Buddhist outlook on life—that all things are illusions, or, to put it in Buddhist terminology, 'colour' (i.e. phenomenon) is the same as 'emptiness' (i.e. nothingness). In contrast to him, both Li Po and Tu Fu use the concrete 'river' and 'mountain' or 'plain' as subjects; therefore their imagery has more reality and solidity. Yet there are differences between these two poets also. Li Po, by using the words 'come to an end' (*chin* 盡) and 'waste' (*huang* 荒), induces a feeling of desolation and solitude, a feeling often exhibited in his poetry and an indication of his egocentric personality. Tu Fu, on the other hand, reveals himself as the observer of life by describing objectively the movements of the stars, the river, and the reflection of the moon in the water. We may further note that Wang Wei dispenses with verbs in his couplet, thus emphasizing the feeling of quietness and unreality; Li Po uses two verbs for each noun ('following' and 'come to an end' for 'mountains'; 'entering' and 'flow' for 'river'), as against Tu Fu's four verbs for four nouns, one for each ('drooping' for 'stars', '(is) vast' for 'plain', 'rushing' for 'moon', and 'flow' for 'river'). Consequently Tu Fu's imagery has greater richness and is more suggestive of movement.

A few more examples may be given from other poets. Kao Shih (700?–765), a contemporary of the above poets, who had a successful career and rose to be Governor-General, shows his masculine character and martial inclinations in such imagery as the following:

> The sound of the rapid flow of the torrent is like arrows,
> The shape of the fading moon over the city is like a bow.

In contrast to the heroic Kao Shih, the poverty-stricken Meng Chiao is fond of describing things as 'cold' or 'thin', such as in

> The shallow well cannot supply my drink,
> The thin fields have long been left unploughed.

Finally, it may be mentioned that the critic Wang Kuo-wei ridiculed the lyric poet Chang Yen (1248–?) of the Sung dynasty, by quoting two images from the latter's poetry: 'Old jade and waste field', punning on Chang Yen's courtesy name, 'Jade-field' (Yü-t'ien). In fact, imagery that reveals a poet's personality approaches the status of personal symbols, which will be discussed below.

Generally speaking, symbols are of two kinds: conventional and private or personal. A conventional symbol is an object chosen by common consent or usage to represent something abstract, such as the rose for Love. It can also be due to a myth or legend, such as the dove as a symbol of peace, because of the Biblical story. In China, there are innumerable conventional symbols, in the language, in pictorial art, and in daily life. Some conventional symbols are due to certain qualities in the objects chosen. For example, the pine-tree is regarded as a symbol of moral fortitude because it withstands rough cold weather, a fact that did not escape the notice of Confucius, who observed, 'It is only in the cold season that one realizes that the pines and cypresses wither last.' Other conventional symbols may owe their origins to puns. For instance, the bat, not a particularly attractive creature, is a symbol of blessing, because both 'bat' and 'blessing' in Chinese are pronounced *fu*. Conventional symbols due to ancient customs, such as willow for parting, or due to legends, such as cuckoo for unhappy love, I have already mentioned before (pp. 11 and 51). Personal symbols are those used by poets to represent a state of mind, a vision of the world, or his own personality. They may be consciously or unconsciously used. Two examples of personal symbolism may be given from Tu Fu's poetry.

The first example is from a poem entitled 'Painted Hawk':

> Wind and frost rise on the white silk:
> The grey hawk is painted with uncommon skill.
> Stretching his body, he wishes for a cunning hare;
> Looking askance, he resembles a sad barbarian.
> His chain and ring are bright, as if touchable;
> From the railings one could almost call him forth.
> When will he attack the common birds,
> Sprinkling their feathers and blood over the wild plain?

No one who has felt the force of the final couplet (in the original at any rate) will be content to take this poem as a mere description of a hawk, and a painted one at that. On the other hand, there is no need to follow the commentator who suggested that the hawk represented the poet while the common birds represented the ubiquitous 'petty men'. The truth may well have been that Tu Fu started in *bona fide* to describe a painted hawk, but the subject so kindled his imagination that the bird became a symbol of heroic strength and violent beauty, rather like Hopkins's windhover:

> Brute beauty and valour and act, oh, air, pride, plume, here
> Buckle!

The other example is from a poem on a horse, containing the lines

> Wherever he goes, space ceases to be;
> To him one can truly entrust one's life.

Here too, one feels the horse has become for Tu Fu, and for us, much more than a horse, but a symbol of certain qualities— courage, loyalty, strength—that the poet admired. Tu Fu's hawk and horse are therefore comparable to Blake's tiger or Hopkins's windhover.

Although Chinese poets use personal symbols as shown above, they seldom use a whole system of personal symbols, as Blake did in his Prophetic Books or Yeats in his later poetry. The poet who made most extensive use of symbolism in Chinese is probably

Ch'ü Yuan.[1] In his *Li Sao* ('Encountering Sorrow'), which describes his sorrow and indignation over his banishment by the King of Ch'u, his search for an ideal woman, his sense of solitude, his grief over the conditions in his native country, and his final despair and resolution to commit suicide, he uses numerous symbols such as flowers, herbs, and mythical figures and animals. Unfortunately, commentators are prone to take these symbols as representing actual persons, thus reducing Ch'ü Yuan's symbolism to the status of allegory. The main difference between symbolism and allegory is easy to perceive. In allegory, there is no difficulty in identifying 'what represents' with 'what is represented'. Indeed, allegory usually consists of personifications of specific virtues and vices (such as in Spenser's *Faerie Queene*), or the reverse—representations of actual persons or institutions in the guise of non-human beings (such as in Dryden's *The Hind and the Panther*). In symbolism, as I mentioned once before, it is not always possible to name what is represented. In other words, a symbol is capable of several interpretations, some of which may be simultaneously acceptable. That is why symbolism has greater richness and subtlety of meaning than allegory. Now, the traditional Chinese commentators on Ch'ü Yuan are often content to work out simple equations between the poet's symbols and actual persons: the orchid = the poet, the weeds = his enemies; the goddess = the king, the suitor = the poet, etc. In this way the whole poem is impoverished. It would be better to take these symbols as representing not definite persons but certain qualities: the orchid and other flowers may be regarded as symbols for various virtues and beauties; the goddess he wishes to marry may be taken as representing ideal beauty and womanhood, while the possibility of its representing ideal kingship as well need not be excluded; the horse and dragon on which the poet rides may be taken as symbols of poetic genius and creative imagination. Seen in this light the poem would appear to possess much wider significance than an allegory.

As I observed earlier, symbolism and imagery are often combined. Not only are symbols and images used together, but the same words can function as both. In the lyric by Wen T'ing-yun quoted on p. 56, the willows, the wild geese, and the fading flowers not only act as imagery to help paint the scene but also symbolize, respectively, parting, exile, and the passage of time. To

[1] See p. 33.

take another example from the same poet, here is a lyric to the tune
P'u-sa Man:

> In the moonlit bower of jade memory of you for ever dwells.
> The silky willow twigs are swinging, soft and weak as spring.
> The grass was growing thick beyond our gate;
> Seeing you off, I heard the horse's neigh.
>
> Behind the curtain gilt with kingfishers,
> The perfumed candle has dissolved in tears.
> Amid the fading flowers and the cuckoo's cries,
> A broken dream still haunts my window green.

Here, various images—the moonlight, the jade bower, the willow
twigs, the curtain, the candle, the flowers, the cuckoo, the green
window—are used to depict the present scene, while others—the
grass, the gate, the horse—are used to recall the past. At the same
time, some of the images are also symbolic: the willow stands for
parting and also a restless state of mind; the candle represents
grief and self-consuming passion; and the cuckoo, as we have
seen before, is a symbol of unhappy love. Thus, imagery and
symbolism are imperceptibly blended, and a dual purpose is ful-
filled by them: to describe an external scene and reveal an inner
emotional experience.

Since imagery and symbolism are often combined, the criteria
suggested earlier for judging the merits of imagery can also be
applied to symbolism. That is to say, whether the symbols used in
a poem are original and personal or conventional, we should ask
what poetic purposes are served by them, and whether they agree
with the context in significance and associations. In the case of
conventional symbols, we should consider how the poet has re-
affirmed, developed, modified, or changed their significance. Just
as poets can use conventional imagery without piling up *clichés*, so
can they use conventional symbols with varying implications and
associations so as to avoid stereotyped repetition. Let us take one
symbol and see how various poets used it: the chrysanthemum.
The earliest use of this flower as a symbol in Chinese poetry that I
know of is by Ch'ü Yuan in the *Li Sao*:

> In the morning I drink the dew drops from the magnolia,
> In the evening I eat the fallen petals of the autumn chrysanthemum.

Here the flower seems to be a symbol of purity and moral in-
tegrity. It may further symbolize longevity, as in the preceding

lines the poet has expressed his apprehension of the coming of old age.

In the *Song of the Autumn Wind* (quoted on p. 50), we recall, the Emperor Wu of Han also used this symbol:

> But the orchids retain their beauty, the chrysanthemums their fragrance yet:
> How they remind me of the lovely lady whom I cannot forget!

In spite of the verbal echoes of Ch'ü Yuan in these lines, the symbolic value of the chrysanthemum is now quite different: it represents feminine beauty here rather than moral integrity. It can also be associated with the idea of longevity, as the song expresses fear of old age and laments the passing of time.

In the hands of T'ao Ch'ien, particularly famed for his fondness of the chrysanthemum, this flower develops into a symbol not only of moral integrity but also of secluded life. He has apotheosized this flower in such lines as these:

> The autumn chrysanthemum has fine colour;
> I pick its beautiful blossoms wet with dew.
> Floating them on the sorrow-chasing wine,
> Further from the world I carry my mind.

Because of its association with T'ao Ch'ien, the chrysanthemum became, as the philosopher Chou Tun-yi remarked in a well-known essay, 'the hermit among flowers'.

However, later poets could still use this flower as a symbol for things other than the life of a hermit. In the following poem by Wang An-shih, its original significance of moral integrity and strength is restored:

> Round, round, the sun over the city:
> The coming of autumn has paled its bright beams.
> The gathering gloom will flood even the sky;
> What chance have insignificant herbs and trees?
> But the yellow chrysanthemum has purest nature,
> Its lone fragrance withstands manifold forces.
> Let me pluck it amid the frost and dew,
> For it is enough to allay one's morning hunger.

In contrast, the poetess Li Ch'ing-chao uses this flower to symbolize wasted youth and faded beauty. In one lyric she writes:

> All over the ground are heaps of yellow flowers:
> Ravaged, haggard, worn.
> Who will pluck them now?

And in another lyric:

> As the curtain rolls up the west wind,
> One is growing thinner than the yellow flowers.

The above examples illustrate how a conventional symbol can be modified in its significance and emotional associations by its context.

3

ALLUSIONS, QUOTATIONS, AND DERIVATIONS

A GREAT deal of Chinese poetry is allusive; it is therefore necessary to pay some attention to the use of allusions as a poetic device. On the whole, there are two kinds of allusions: general and specific. General allusions are those made to common knowledge and beliefs, such as allusions in Chinese poetry to the five elements (metal, wood, water, fire, and earth); to the two contrasting principles of Nature, *yin* and *yang*; to astronomy and astrology, etc. These are comparable to allusions in European poetry, especially Mediaeval and Renaissance poetry, to the four elements, the four humours, astronomy and astrology, etc. Specific allusions are those made to particular literary works, historical events and persons, legends, and myths. The boundary line between the two kinds of allusions is a shifting one; for what may be taken for granted in one age as common knowledge may become in another age recondite, and conversely, originally specific allusions may, through repeated use, become part and parcel of the language. For instance, allusions to Confucian classics in Chinese poetry, which would have been readily understood by all literate Chinese in the old days, may present difficulties to a contemporary Chinese reader, just as classical allusions in English poetry, which would have caused no obscurity to an Elizabethan or eighteenth-century English reader, may do so to a modern one. On the other hand, some allusive compounds in Chinese, such as 'wish to study' for 'fifteen years old',[1] have long become conventional expressions no longer intended to contain specific references, just as certain English idioms of Biblical origin, such as 'olive branch', are no longer used as specific allusions. In a society where most readers may be presumed to have a similar educational background, such as in ancient China or Renaissance Europe, the poet can use allusions with greater confidence, in the same way as he may use conventional symbols. In an age such as the present one, when no common body of knowledge and beliefs can be taken for granted among all readers, allusions tend to appear obscure, like private symbols. This analogy between allusions and symbols can be carried into the field of practical criticism. As in dealing with symbols, so in dealing with allusions we should ask not so much whether they are original or conventional, popular or abstruse, but rather whether they have any purpose or justification. In other words, we should ask: Does this allusion add anything to the total poetic effect or does it simply show off the poet's learning? Is there any reason for using allusions here, or could the poet have expressed what is embodied in the allusions just as well without using them? Such, I suggest, should be the criteria for judging the merits of allusions in poetry. There is no need to condemn all allusions as pedantic and artificial, as some critics have done. All we need to consider is how an allusion is used, so as to find out if it is justified or necessitated by any reason. The following are some reasons that may justify or necessitate the use of allusions.

First, allusions can be used as an economical means of presenting a situation. They can act as a kind of shorthand to communicate to the reader certain facts which would otherwise require explanation and take up space. For example, in a poem written late in life, Tu Fu wrote:

> Yü Hsin's whole life was nothing but bleakness,
> But in his last years his poetry moved the River Pass.[2]

Yü Hsin (513–581) was a poet whom Tu Fu admired and to whose poetry he once compared Li Po's as a compliment to the latter, as we have seen (p. 107). Yü lived during the Southern and Northern Dynasties, and though a native of the south, he was forcibly detained in the north and served the northern court against his will.

---

[1] See above, p. 7.
[2] A stretch of the Yangtze River flanked by mountains.

His poetry therefore often shows regret and nostalgia. By alluding to him, Tu Fu suggested that he himself was also living in times of trouble and far from home, and that he too could only find consolation in the thought that his poetic achievements might recompense to some extent what he had missed in life in other respects. Had Tu Fu not used an allusion but simply written, 'My whole life has been nothing but bleakness, but now in my old age my poetry is moving the River Pass', he would have appeared to be indulging in self-pity and self-conceit. Of course, this kind of allusion can easily become *clichés*, so that every frustrated poet fancies himself a misunderstood genius like Ch'ü Yuan or Li Po, and every unhappy young lady is compared to a neglected Empress or wronged beauty. However, such abuses of allusions cannot vitiate their proper use in poetry.

Sometimes, instead of drawing an analogy between a past event and the present situation in the poem, an allusion can provide a contrast. The effect can be tragic, comic, or ironic, as the case may be. In a poem written while separated from his wife and family during the rebellion of An Lu-shan, Tu Fu writes:

> The Cowherd and the Spinning Maid need not grieve,
> At least they can cross the river every autumn!

The legend alluded to is briefly as follows. The Spinning Maid, a daughter of the Emperor of Heaven, married the Cowherd, a common mortal. She grew homesick and ran back to heaven, whereupon he pursued her but was stopped by the Heavenly River (i.e. the Milky Way). However, they are allowed to cross the river once a year, on the seventh day of the Seventh Moon, when all the magpies in the air would assemble to form a bridge for them. The poet here contrasts his own indefinite separation from his wife with the mythical couple's happy annual reunion, so as to bring out the hopelessness of his situation.

The use of allusions as a means of presenting a situation is particularly effective in dramatic poetry. In *The Girl Whose Soul Left Her Body*, the heroine's soul leaves her body, runs away from home, and overtakes her fiancé who is on his way to the capital. When she (the disembodied soul) asks him to take her with him, he questions the propriety of such conduct. Thereupon she replies:

> If you should become like Chia Yi stranded at Ch'ang-sha,
> I would undertake to be as virtuous as Meng Kuang.

Chia Yi was a scholar of the Han dynasty, who became renowned in early life but was banished to Ch'ang-sha. Meng Kuang was the exemplary wife of Liang Hung, another scholar of the same dynasty. By alluding to them the hereoine pledges her faith and pays the young man a compliment at the same time. Later she tells him again:

> Like Chuo Wen-chün selling wine at Lin-ch'iung,
> I would wait on you, Ssŭ-ma who wrote on the bridge over
> the Wash-brocade River.

Chuo Wen-chün was a rich young widow who eloped with the scholar Ssŭ-ma Hsiang-ju and who, in their poverty, served wine in an inn to make a living. The heroine of the play thus shows her resolution to follow her fiancé to the end of the earth and to share his hardships. The second line alludes to the story that Ssŭ-ma Hsiang-ju, when setting out to seek his fortune, wrote on a pillar of the bridge over the Wash-brocade River (Chuo-chin Chiang): 'I will never cross this bridge again unless in a carriage drawn by four horses.' This allusion is also apposite, as the hero of the play is on his way to the capital to try his luck at the imperial examination. Such allusions are frequently used in Chinese poetic drama, especially at the meetings of young lovers, who often allude to famous lovers of the past, in the same way as do Lorenzo and Jessica in *The Merchant of Venice*.

The story of Chuo Wen-chün and Ssŭ-ma Hsiang-ju is also alluded to in the *Romance of the Western Chamber*, but this time the allusion points at a contrast and creates a comic and ironic effect. The heroine has made an appointment with the hero, but when he comes she reproaches him and leaves. The maid-servant then says to the disappointed young man:

> Henceforth Chuo Wen-Chün will be penitent;
> And you, my dear Ssŭ-ma, go back and learn to woo!

A more subtle kind of irony is achieved by the following allusion in *Autumn in the Han Palace*. When the Emperor sits alone at night after his favourite has gone to Mongolia, he hears some court musicians playing:

> Hark, at the Court of Heavenly Music, they are playing the
> phoenix-pipes!
> Ah, tell me no more this is the *Hsiao-shao* in nine parts!

A moment later, he hears a solitary wild goose crying, which makes him feel even more depressed. As the *Hsiao-shao* is alleged to have been the music of the sage Emperor Shun, which attracted happy pairs of phoenixes dancing to the court, the allusion here shows an ironic contrast: instead of the phoenixes, the music now only heralds the advent of a lonely wild goose.

In some dramatic poetry, allusions to analogous situations and those providing contrasts are used side by side. In *The Sophisticated Maid*, the hero, going to a secret tryst with his lady-love in the garden, feels nervous. To encourage him, the maid says:

> This is surely a Peach-blossom Fountain where flowers bloom
> in the bright sunshine,
> It is unlike the fire at the Hsien Temple spreading its smoke
> far and wide!

The former of these allusions is to the well-known story of Liu Ch'en and Juan Chao who met two lady immortals at the Peach-blossom Fountain and lived with them. The latter is to a little known story and requires a longer explanation. Hsien is the Chinese name for Zoroastrianism, and the 'fire at the Hsien Temple' alludes to the following story. The Emperor of Shu had a daughter, whose nurse had a son of the same age. The two children were brought up together in the palace, until they came of age. Naturally the young man had to leave the palace, whereupon he fell lovesick for the princess. Learning this, the princess agreed to meet him in secret at the Zoroastrian Temple. The young man arrived first, but fell asleep. Then came the princess, who, failing to wake him up, went away and left him a love-token. Soon the young man awoke, and realized what he had missed. So great was his remorse that it turned into a blaze which consumed him as well as the temple. This bizarre tale must have been popular in Yuan times, for it is alluded to in four other plays of this period, including the *Romance of the Western Chamber*, and indeed there was a play, now lost, entitled *The Fire at the Hsien Temple*. In the lines quoted above, the allusion to this story signifies a clandestine love affair with a tragic ending, in contrast to the Peach-blossom Fountain, which represents a happy romantic liaison.

Whether allusions are used to reveal an analogy or a contrast, they add the authority of past experience to the present occasion, and hence strengthen the poetic effect. Moreover, by calling up a chain of associations with the past, they can build up an extra dimension of meaning and extend the significance of the present context. They are therefore not a lazy substitute for description and narrative but a means of introducing additional implications and associations.

Furthermore, there may be practical reasons for using allusions, such as when a clandestine love affair is involved, or when political or personal satire is intended. Under such circumstances allusions afford an obvious way of avoiding scandal or prosecution.

In short, the use of allusions is a justifiable poetic device, provided they are not intended as a display of erudition but as an organic part of the total poetic design. Like imagery and symbolism, allusions can effectively and economically body forth certain feelings and situations, evoke various association and extend the terms of reference of the poem.

Since allusions, imagery, and symbolism resemble one another in function, they are often combined in usage. The force of an image or symbol can be enhanced if it is associated with an allusion. In a poem on peonies damaged by rain, Li Shang-yin uses this image:

Again and again tears are sprinkled on the jade plate.

Here the raindrops on the white peonies are compared to tears on a jade plate. Further, the image contains an allusion to the story that when a mermaid said farewell to her host, she shed tears, which turned into pearls, on a jade plate. The allusion therefore introduces a new complication to the image: in addition to being compared to tears, the raindrops are now implicitly compared to pearls as well. And of course the whole image might be more than a description of rain on peonies, but a symbol of something of greater significance—ravaged beauty or frustrated genius, perhaps. The same allusion is used in another poem of Li Shang-yin's, one without title and probably written in memory of his deceased wife:

By the vast sea, pearls have tears in the bright moonlight.

This time the comparison is reversed: instead of describing tears as pearls, the poet does the opposite, so as to emphasize the feeling of sadness: even pearls are crying, let alone the poet himself. A world seen under the light of 'Pathetic Fallacy' is thus revealed.

In cases like the above, the image is the dominating factor in the line, while the allusion acts as a subsidiary factor. In other cases, the allusion is the dominating factor, but once introduced, it cannot help becoming an image or symbol at the same time. In another poem by Li Shang-yin, probably written for a Taoist nun, the poet alludes to the legend of Ch'ang O, who stole her husband King Yi's elixir of life and fled to the moon:

> Ch'ang O should regret having stolen the elixir;
> Nightly she faces the green sea and blue sky alone!

The poet's primary intention is to suggest that the nun in her solitude may regret having taken the vow of chastity, as Ch'ang O might be supposed to regret having renounced human love for the sake of gaining immortality, but the figure of the goddess, once introduced, also becomes a description of the nun's beauty in moonlight. The allusion, therefore, involves an image as a consequence.

As Li Shang-yin's poetry is particularly rich in allusions as well as imagery and symbolism, let us take two complete poems of his among those labelled 'Without Title', and see how all three devices, together with others, are used to weave a total poetic texture. These poems without titles are notoriously obscure; nevertheless, we can reconstruct, from details in the poems themselves and what we know of the poet's life, a situation for each poem, in the context of which a consistent reading may be arrived at. The first poem I have quoted once before for its metre (p. 28), but for the sake of convenience I will repeat the translation here:

> Hard it is for us to meet and hard to go away;
> Powerless lingers the eastern wind as all the flowers decay.
> The spring silkworm will only end his thread when death befalls;
> The candle will drip with tears until it turns to ashes grey.
> Facing the morning mirror, she fears her cloudy hair will fade;
> Reading poems by night, she should be chilled by the moon's ray.
> The fairy mountain P'eng lies at no great distance:
> May a Blue Bird fly to her and my tender cares convey!

We may take this poem as an expression of the poet's love for a woman who lives within easy reach but with whom for some reason he cannot openly communicate. In the first line, the word 'hard' is used in two slightly different senses: not only is it hard (i.e. difficult) for the lovers to meet, but once having met they find it hard (i.e. unbearable) to part. It is possible this line has an additional meaning, that one of them is going away and it is hard for them even to contrive to meet and say good-bye to each other. In the second line, the powerless wind probably represents the poet, while the flowers represent his beloved: he is as powerless to prevent her youth and beauty from passing away as the wind is to stop the flowers withering away. At the same time, these images also serve the more immediate purpose of describing the actual scenery and the time of the year. In the next two lines, two more images are introduced. Just as the silkworm imprisons itself in the cocoon formed by its own endless silk, so does the poet enwrap himself in the endless sorrow of his own making; and just as the candle is consumed by its own heat, so is the poet by his unfulfilled passion. These images are further enriched by auditory associations. In line 3, the word for 'silk-thread' and that for 'death' are both pronounced *ssŭ* (*si* in Ancient Chinese), though not in the same tone. This can hardly be fortuitous in such a highly conscious artist as Li Shang-yin. The homophones are probably intended to bring closer the image of the silkworm with the idea of death. Moreover, the word 'silk-thread' (*ssŭ*) is often used to depict endless, unbreakable love, or endless thoughts of sorrow, the word for 'thought' being also pronounced *ssŭ* (*si* in Ancient Chinese). It would therefore not be too fanciful to associate 'silk-thread' here with such compounds as 'love-thread' (*ch'ing-ssŭ*, i.e. endless love) or 'sorrow-thread' (= thoughts)', (*ch'ou-ssŭ*: 愁 絲 or 愁 思). In line 4, the word for 'ashes', *huei*, as I suggested before (p. 12), may be associated with 'ash hearted' (*huei-hsin*, i.e. despair). In the next couplet, the poet imagines how his beloved sits alone at night, fearing the passing away of her youth and feeling lonely in the cold moonlight. It is tempting to associate this picture of a lady feeling lonely in the moonlight with the other poem suggesting that the lady in the moon, Ch'ang O, should regret having stolen the elixir of life, and to suppose that both poems are written for the same Taoist nun. This possibility is strengthened by the two Taoist allusions in the final couplet: the fairy mountain P'eng, dwelling of Taoist immortals and a symbol of bliss, and the Blue Bird, a messenger that heralded the arrival of the Queen Mother of the Western Heavens (Hsi Wang Mu), a Taoist goddess, to the court of the Emperor Wu of Han. Be that as it may, the whole poem is built up with images, symbols, and allusions, which present a coherent picture and reveal a frustrated passion.

The second poem describes a young lady's futile preparation for her wedding and her longings for the absent lover:

The fragrant silk, 'Phoenix-tail', lies in thin folds;
The green-patterned round top is being sewn in the depth of night.
Her fan, cut from the moon's soul, cannot hide her shame;
His carriage, rolling past like thunder, allowed no time for talk.
In solitude she has watched the golden flickers grow dim;
No news will ever come to announce the Red Pomegranate Wine!
The piebald horse is always tied to a willow by the river;
Where can one wait for the good south-west wind?

This admittedly does not make much sense without explanation, but neither does the original to the uninitiated reader. Tedious and laborious as they may be, explanations on allusions, imagery, and symbolism are necessary for such a poem. After all, some modern Western poems require no less elucidation, and if a reader has the patience to read commentaries on modern Western poems, he should be prepared to take similar pains with ancient Chinese ones. In this poem, the images in the first two lines are simple ones, giving a description of the bed-curtain for the bridal chamber, made of thin 'Phoenix-tail' silk, with a round top. The lady is busy sewing this in the hope of celebrating her wedding soon. In line 3, the white circular fan is compared to the moon—a compound image which involves several allusions. First, the image is derived from a song of complaint by Lady Pan, a court lady of the Han dynasty, in which she compares the circular fan to the moon, and herself, having lost Imperial favour, to the fan discarded in autumn when it is no longer needed. The allusion therefore suggests a lady deserted by her lover. Secondly, among the Music Department songs,[1] there is one called 'White Circular Fan', which is said to have originated in the following manner. Wang Min of the Chin dynasty carried on a love affair with his sister-in-law's maid, named Hsieh Fang-tzǔ. One day, when the sister-in-law was caning the maid heavily, Wang asked her to stop. Knowing that the maid was a good singer, the sister-in-law demanded her to sing in lieu of further punishment. Thereupon Hsieh sang:

White circular fan!
The hardships and bitterness you've gone through
Have all been seen by your young man.

[1] See p. 33.

139

and again:

> White circular fan,
> Haggard and worn, unlike in days of old,
> You are ashamed to see your young man!

This allusion adds the idea of shame to that of desertion. Finally, the image can be associated with Ch'ang O, the lady in the moon, to whom allusion is made in the other two poems quoted above. In line 4, the comparison of the sound of the carriage to thunder alludes to two lines in Ssŭ-ma Hsiang-ju's *Song of the Long Gate* (*Ch'ang Men Fu*), written on behalf of the Empress Ch'en when she was living at the Palace of Long Gate after having lost the Emperor Wu's favour. The allusion thus further emphasizes the idea of desertion. However, the *Song of the Long Gate* so moved the Emperor that the Empress was restored to his favour, and the allusion may therefore suggest a hope for a similar return to favour. In line 5, the 'golden flickers' refers to a candle burning out and may be taken both as a simple image describing a lonely night and as a symbol of despair. In line 6, the Red Pomegranate Wine means the wine for the wedding night and harks back to nuptial preparations carried out against hope. Line 7 alludes to another Music Department song about a young man riding on a piebald horse, who roamed abroad and would not go home. It further alludes, by mentioning the willow, to 'plucking the willow at Chang Terrace', a conventional euphemism for visiting a courtesan. The implications of these two allusions are that the absent lover is wandering about and that the young lady suspects him of having been detained in the company of some singing girl. The last line alludes to two lines in a poem by Ts'ao Chih (192–232), put in the mouth of a deserted wife:

> I wish to become the south-west wind
> To fly far away, into your arms.

By means of the above allusions, images, and symbolism, the poet expresses the young lady's complex feeling of hope, sorrow, indignation, shame, suspicion, and frustration. The allusions are the main means to bring out the underlying meaning, yet because they are combined with imagery, they do not appear pedantic and prosaic. The images, on the other hand, create a physical background for the emotions expressed. They are highly sensuous, appealing to several senses. Some of them contain explicit colour descriptions: the green silk curtain, the golden flickers, the red pomegranate wine, the piebald horse; others imply colour: the white fan, the green willow. These colours, together with the shapes of the phoenix tails on the silk, the round top of the curtain, and the circular fan, appeal to the visual sense. At the same time, the silk, being both fragrant and thin, also appeals to the olfactory and tactile senses. For sound, there is the carriage rolling by like thunder; for taste, the pomegranate wine.

The above two poems represent Chinese poetry of the 'oblique' kind at its extreme. They illustrate how rich, complex, subtle, and condensed Chinese poetry can be, in revealing different worlds of experience through an integration of imagery, symbolism, and allusions.

A practice closely akin to the use of allusions is that of quotations, either from previous poets or other sources. In fact, a quotation differs from a specific allusion only in the extent to which the original writing is repeated.

Owing to considerations of space, quotations are less common than allusions in short poems, except when 'collecting lines' (*chi chü* 集 句) is practised, in which case lines from different poems are gleaned to form a whole new poem. This practice, which somewhat resembles arranging traditional melodies for orchestration, requires great skill, extensive reading, and strong memory. But in the last analysis it is really a *jeu d'esprit* rather than serious poetry, for it involves no original writing at all. A more serious use of quotations is to integrate them with the rest of the poem. For instance, a lyric by Hsin Ch'i-chi (1140–1207) begins with the line,

> Alas, how much have I aged,

and ends with

> The only ones who know me
> Are you two or three gentlemen.

Now the first line is a quotation from the Confucian *Analects*, and the expression 'you two or three gentlemen' in the last line is also used by Confucius several times. These quotations are woven into the texture of the poem, which expresses the poet's philosophical outlook on life in his old age. They may further suggest a wish to emulate the wisdom of the Master quoted.

By far the most important use of quotations occurs in poetic drama. Here, quotations can be used for various purposes. To begin with, the dramatic poet can quote a line from another poet to describe the present scene or the feelings of a character. In *Li K'uei's Apology* (*Li K'uei Fu-ching*) by K'ang Chin-chih (thirteenth century), the hero, a rough outlaw, quotes a line from Tu Fu:

Debts owed for wine are common, incurred everywhere I go.

The same poet is quoted by a singing girl in *The Gold-thread Pond*:

A flight of fading flowers bears spring away.

As a matter of fact, these are simply cases of borrowing, and there is no need for the audience or reader to recognize the quotation as such. No more are we supposed to believe that the outlaw and singing girl could know Tu Fu by heart than we are asked to believe that a fourteenth-century Scythian conqueror could quote an Elizabethan poet.[1]

Then, there are times when it is necessary for the audience or reader to recognize quotations in order to perceive their significance, even if the character may not be represented as consciously quoting. In *The Sophisticated Maid*, the young lovers are forced to separate by the girl's mother, but eventually the hero, having come first at the imperial examination, returns to marry the girl by the Emperor's order. His true identity is concealed from the girl's family, who are merely told that it is the Emperor's wish that the new *chuang-yuan* (first among successful candidates) should marry the young lady. When at last the maid-servant discovers who the bridegroom-to-be really is, she tells her young mistress:

To-night, 'an old friend has come from far away'!

This quotation from the opening section of the Confucian *Analects* is extremely well known, but now it assumes an altogether different significance. In such cases, the dramatic poet deliberately gives a twist to the meaning of the quotation by putting it in an unexpected context, and it is necessary for us to realize this. The effect can be comic or ironic, depending on the situation. Such uses of quotations are comparable to Shakespeare's comic use of 'I came, saw, and overcame' in *As You Like It*, or Marlowe's

[1] Marlowe, *Tamburlaine*, Part II, Act IV, Sc. iii, 119–24; Spenser, *Faerie Queene*, Book 1, Canto vii, V. 32.

ironic use of Ovid's *Amores* in *Doctor Faustus*, where the doomed sinner borrows the words of the ardent lover to wish for prolonged night: *O lente, lente currite, noctis equi!*

Finally, the dramatic poet can of course represent a character as consciously quoting. This may be done for two different reasons: either to show the character of the speaker by what he quotes, or to stress a character's pedantry by putting into his mouth abundant quotations. An example of a quotation illustrating the character of the speaker is the following proverb quoted by the villain Mao Yen-shou in *Autumn in the Han Palace*:

> He is no gentleman who cannot hate deeply,
> Nor is he a hero who bears no malice.

As for the use of quotations as a means to show the pedantry of a character, this device is exploited to the full in *The Sophisticated Maid*. In this play, both the lovers are pedantic and often resort to quotations. To make them appear even more comic, the author lets the maid Fan Su, who is the real heroine of the play as the title indicates, beat the lovers at their own game. When Fan Su pleads on behalf of the lovesick young man, the young lady affects indifference and quotes from the *Analects*:

> This is a case of 'a man without the virtues proper to mankind'; why should I save him?

In reply, Fan Su quotes from the same book:

> 'I do not know how a person who does not keep his promise is to get on',

and goes on to reproach her young mistress for failing to keep her promise to the young man. Throughout the play, there are no less than eighteen quotations from the *Analects*, three from the *Mencius*, two from the *Tao Tê Ching*, and one from a Buddhist sutra. These greatly add to the comic effect by stressing the pedantry of the lovers and the mock-pedantry of the maid. That the dramatist intended them for such a purpose may be seen from the following remarks he has put into the mouth of Fan Su. When the young man pays his first visit to the young lady's mother, the hostess and the guest emulate each other in polite and learned conversation. Thereupon Fan Su comments:

> They have exchanged but a few words in conversation,
> Yet in doing so almost discussed all the nine classics!

Again, when the young lady refuses to go out into the garden and insists on studying, saying,

> The Sage said, 'At fifteen I set my mind on studying',

the maid says in an aside,

> What could you do with someone so crazy?

It is clear from these remarks that the author is not showing off his own learning (for which purpose it would require much more than quoting from such familiar books as the *Analects*, at any rate), but is making fun of his characters. The charge of pedantry made against the dramatist by two critics of the Ch'ing dynasty, Li T'iao-yuan and Liang T'ing-nan, is based on a failure to see the dramatic function of quotations in this play.

Instead of quoting or alluding to other writers, a poet can derive an idea or an expression from another. We have already seen how one can use derived imagery and symbols; similar derivations can be made in conception, in the use of epithets, etc. A great deal of Chinese poetry is derivative, but this does not necessarily mean it is poor poetry. Rather than condemning all derivative poetry, we should ask whether a poet has modified his 'sources' to suit his own poetic purpose, or is simply copying slavishly. No one can write poetry in Chinese as if Ch'ü Yuan, Tu Fu, Wang Wei, Li Po, and many others had not written, no more than one can write poetry in English as if Shakespeare, Milton, and many others had never written. As Mr. T. S. Eliot observed, 'in poetry there is no such thing as complete originality owing nothing to the past'. We should, therefore, not demand absolute originality, but assess the merits of a poem in the context of the whole poetic tradition to which it belongs. On the other hand, we should not err in the opposite direction by following some Chinese commentators who seem to regard derivation as a virtue in itself. Such commentators, in their over-zealous search for 'sources', are apt to see derivations where none really exist. Give them a line, 'How brightly the moon shines', and they will cite you 'Brightly rises the moon' from *The Book of Poetry* as its source. It has even been alleged that every single word in Tu Fu's poetry is derived from some literary source—an allegation which was made as a compliment to the poet's learning but which, if true, would deprive him of any claim to creative genius.

In brief, Chinese poetry, especially later poetry, is often not original in theme or in individual expressions, yet such poetry is not all worthless. This statement does not contradict my general thesis that poetry is an exploration of language, for a poem that uses derived ideas and expressions can yet be original in the way these ideas and expressions are put together. In other words, a derivative poem can be good if it succeeds in integrating borrowed ideas and expressions into a new pattern. Chinese poets often use conventional phrases, images, and symbols as Byzantine artists used bits of coloured glass and stones for mosaics: their originality lies not in the material used but in the final result achieved.

4

ANTITHESIS

———

T HERE is a natural tendency in Chinese towards antithesis.
For instance, instead of saying 'size', one says 'big-small-
ness' (*ta-hsiao*), and instead of 'landscape', one says 'mountain-
waters' (*shan-shuei*). Such expressions, as I remarked before, re-
veal a dualistic and relativistic way of thinking. Moreover, mono-
syllabic words and disyllabic compounds, which constitute the
bulk of the language, lend themselves easily to antithesis. For
example, 'river' (*chiang*) and 'mountain' (*shan*) form an antithesis;
so do 'flower' (*hua*) and 'bird' (*niao*). These two antithetical pairs
can then be used to form another antithesis: 'river and mountain'
(*chiang shan*) in contrast to 'flower and bird' (*hua niao*). It is easy to
form a tetrasyllabic phrase with two antithetical disyllabic com-
pounds: 'red flower and green leaves' (*hung-hua lü-yeh*), 'blue sky
and white sun' (*ch'ing-t'ien pai-jih*), and such like. Such being the
case with the language itself, it is inevitable that antithesis should
play an important part in Chinese poetry.

Before we examine the use of antithesis in Chinese poetry, it
should be pointed out that antithesis, known as *tuei* in Chinese,
differs from 'parallelism', such as in Hebrew poetry. Antithesis
consists of strict antonyms, allowing no repetition of the same
words, as parallelism does. Take the following verse from the
Song of Solomon:

> Thy teeth are like a flock of sheep that are even shorn, which came
> up from the washing; . . .
> Thy lips are like a thread of scarlet. . . .

146

Thy neck is like the tower of David. . . .
Thy two breasts are like two young does that are twins, which feed
among the lilies.

Here the objects enumerated are meant to show the various charms
of the beloved, not to draw attention to any contrasting qualities;
and the repetition of the words 'thy' and 'like' would be quite
inadmissible in Chinese antithetical couplets.

Antithesis, often of a loose kind, is found in early Chinese
poetry, such as *The Book of Poetry* and *The Songs of Ch'u*. The lines
quoted from the *Li Sao* on p. 128 may be given again as an illus-
tration:

In the morning I drink the dew drops from the magnolia,
In the evening I eat the fallen petals of the autumn chrysanthe-
mum.

The repetition of the words 'in the' and 'I' in the translation does
not occur in the original, where the subject is understood and no
preposition is needed before 'morning' and 'evening'. The only
repetition that does occur is that of the possessive particle *chih*
('of'). Apart from that, another feature which renders the anti-
thesis a little inexact is the use of a disyllabic compound *mu-lan*
('magnolia') to contrast with an adjective plus a noun, *ch'iu chü*
('autumn chrysanthemum').

In Ancient Verse, antithesis often occurs, but is neither
obligatory nor strict, as in Regulated Verse. For instance, in a
poem in Ancient Verse by Li Po, the opening lines run:

The Yellow River flows to the eastern main,
The white sun sets over the western sea.

This is not a strictly antithetical couplet. First, 'Yellow River' and
'white sun', in spite of their verbal contrast, do not really form an
exact antithesis, for the one is a proper name while the other is
not. Secondly, 'main' (*ming*) and 'sea' (*hai*) are synonyms rather
than antonyms. Lastly, there is no tonal contrast between the
syllables of the two lines (which of course does not show in the
translation).

In Regulated Verse, antithesis is demanded by the versification.
As I mentioned before, the four middle lines of an eight-line poem
in Regulated Verse should form two antithetical couplets, con-
trasting with each other in sense as well as in sound. In an anti-
thetical couplet, each syllable in the first line should contrast in

tone with the corresponding syllable in the next line, as shown in the tone patterns on pp. 26 and 27. At the same time, the contrasted words should be of the same grammatical category: noun against noun, verb against verb, etc. This is not always strictly observed, especially among earlier writers of Regulated Verse. Wang Po (647–675), an early T'ang poet, for instance, wrote:

> *Yü chün li-pieh yi*
> With you parting-separation feeling
> *T'ung shih huan-yu jen*
> Together are official-travelling men
> (I am moved while parting from you,
> Both obliged to travel in official life.)

The contrast between *yü chün* ('with you') and *t'ung shih* ('together are') is far from being exact. Likewise Wang Wei wrote:

> *Liu-shuei ju yu yi*
> Flowing-water seems have feeling
> *Mu-ch'in hsiang yü huan*
> Evening birds mutually joining return
> (The flowing water seems to have feeling,
> The evening birds join together in return.)

Here, the words *ju yu yi* ('seems have feeling') are contrasted with *hsiang yü huan* ('mutually joining return'): verb + verb + noun contrasted with adverb + verb + verb. Such couplets are not considered as skilful as one in which the contrast is grammatical as well as semantic, like a couplet of Tu Fu's quoted once before:

> *Ch'an-sheng chi ku-ssŭ*
> Cicada sound gather ancient temple
> *Niao-ying tu han-t'ang*
> Bird shadow cross cold pond
> (Cicada's cries gather in the ancient temple,
> A bird's shadow crosses the cold pond.)

In both lines the grammatical structure is: noun + noun + verb + adjective + noun.

Furthermore, the words which contrast with each other should refer to the same category of things. Again, this is not always observed, but the more closely the 'referents' of the words belong together in Nature, the more skilful the antithesis is supposed to be. One should contrast colour with colour, flower with flower, etc. Thus, 'moon' and 'star' would form a better antithesis than, say, 'moon' and 'house'. This is one of the reasons why Tu Fu's couplet

> The *stars* drooping, the wild plain (is) vast;
> The *moon* rushing, the great river flows

is particularly admired.

However, two words which do not refer to objects of the same kind but are often mentioned together, such as 'flower and bird' or 'poetry and wine', when separated and contrasted with one another, are also considered particularly skilful. In another couplet by Tu Fu, 'flowers' and 'birds' are used in antithesis:

> Moved by the times, the *flowers* are shedding tears;
> Averse to parting, the *birds* are stricken to the soul.

Traditional handbooks on versification give lists of categories of objects for use in antithesis: astronomy, geography, flora, fauna, etc.[1] Such categories, mechanical and arbitrary as they are, illustrate a reasonable enough principle of contrasting things of the same kind, though they need not be taken too seriously as a criterion to judge the merits of antithetical couplets.

Antithesis also occurs in Lyric Metres and Dramatic Verse, though not as commonly as in Regulated Verse, due to the fact that in Lyric and Dramatic Metres the lines are often not of the same length, which renders strict antithesis impossible. Nevertheless, in some metres containing two successive lines of the same length, antithesis is habitually used. For instance, the first two lines of the second stanza in the *Huan Hsi Sha* are usually antithetical, such as in the poem in this metre by Li Ch'ing-chao quoted on p. 51:

> The new shoots have grown into bamboos beneath the steps;
> The fallen flowers have all gone into the swallows' nests near by.

Sometimes antithesis is used in both stanzas that make up a lyric. In the *T'a So Hsing* ('Treading on Grass'), the first two lines of both stanzas are antithetical. A poem in this metre by Yen Shu (991–1055), from whom, incidentally, the present writer is descended on the maternal side, begins with the lines:

> Little path strewn with red,
> Fragrant fields filled with green.

---

[1] For those who can read Chinese, there is a detailed list of such categories in Wang Li's *Han-yü Shih-lü Hsüeh*, pp. 153–66.

This antithesis is echoed by the first two lines of the second stanza:

> Emerald leaves hide the oriole,
> Vermilion curtain bars the swallow.

The following are a few examples of antithesis in Dramatic Verse. In *Autumn in the Han Palace*, before the Emperor has met the beautiful Wang Chao-chün, he imagines a neglected lady in the palace:

> The shades of bamboos that shake without a wind
> Make her suspect my presence;
> The light of the moon that tinges the gauze of her window
> Fills her heart with grief.

And in the final scene of this play, when he sits alone in the palace after she has gone to Mongolia, he feels the loneliness of his situation:

> Under the painted eaves the 'iron horses'[1] are clanging,
> In the precious hall the imperial couch is cold.
> The falling leaves rustle in the chilly night,
> The candle glimmers in the silent palace.

In *Li K'uei's Apology*, at the beginning of the play, the author describes the scene in antithetical lines:

> The mild wind gradually rises,
> The evening rain has just stopped.
> The willow trees half hide the wine shop,
> The peach blossoms brightly shine on the fishing boats.

To sum up: antithesis is an important and characteristic poetic device in Chinese. Like any other device, it can be abused, and when it is, it degenerates into a mechanical pairing off of words. But at its best it can reveal a perception of the underlying contrasting aspects of Nature and simultaneously strengthen the structure of the poem. The perfect antithetical couplet is natural, not forced, and though the two lines form a sharp contrast, they yet somehow seem to possess a strange affinity, like two people of opposite temperaments happily married, so that one might remark of the couplet, as of the couple, 'What a contrast, yet what a perfect match!'

[1] Bells hanging under the eaves.

EPILOGUE

———

In the preceding pages we have gone a long way in search of answers to the questions raised at the beginning of the book. We have examined the nature of the Chinese language as a poetic medium from various angles; we have discussed different schools of Chinese criticism, and derived from them a view of poetry which provided the main criteria for Chinese poetry. We have also applied systematically the method of verbal analysis to imagery, symbolism, and other poetic devices in Chinese. Such analysis, when carried out in conjunction with the other aspects of language discussed in the first part of this volume (visual and auditory effects, implications and associations of words, grammatical structure, and underlying concepts), should prove a reliable basis for critical evaluation.

There have been a number of poems scattered throughout the book as illustrations. The choice of these poems, while influenced to some extent by personal taste and even memory (for as a rule I quote and translate only poems I know by heart), has not been entirely haphazard, but made with a view to redressing the somewhat biased conception of Chinese poetry that seems to exist among some English-speaking readers—that Chinese poetry is simple, straightforward, and rather flat in language, and restrained and philosophical in tone. The poems I have chosen have shown, I hope, that Chinese poetry is in theme as often romantic as philosophical; in feeling as often passionate as restrained; in language more often subtle and complex than simple and direct; and in form generally written in strict metres and not in the kind of loose rimeless verse that easily lends itself to such parodies as those with which Sir Alan Herbert has occasionally graced the pages of *Punch*.

Epilogue

The Western reader should also be reminded that the majority of Chinese poems, in spite of their having been written in different centuries, have a contemporaneity for Chinese readers. This is due to the fact that the Chinese written language has changed little during the last two thousand years or so. Naturally the pronunciation of words has changed, and their use has become increasingly complex, but the actual written characters have not changed. Hence the bulk of Chinese poetry can be, and is, read and enjoyed without too much effort. Difficult poems of course exist, but their difficulty is usually attributable to obscure allusions and personal symbolism rather than archaic language. It requires less philological knowledge to read ancient Chinese than classical or mediaeval European poetry, and at a guess I would say that there are more Chinese readers who read *The Book of Poetry* (cir. twelfth to seventh centuries B.C.) for pleasure than there are English-speaking ones who read *Beowulf* (seventh century A.D.) for the same purpose. The Western reader should therefore readjust his sense of historical perspective while reading Chinese poetry, and refuse to be misled by the dates of the poems into thinking that they are remote in feeling and expression in proportion to their degree of antiquity. As a matter of fact, most Chinese readers are far more familiar with poets of the T'ang dynasty (seventh to tenth centuries) than those, say, of the Ming dynasty (fourteenth to seventeenth centuries).

Having nearly reached the end of my task, I may now perhaps be allowed the indulgence of some general reflections on Chinese poetry. On the whole, Chinese poetry excels in short lyric and reflective verse, but is relatively weak in narrative verse. Of course narrative poems do exist, but they never exceed a few hundred lines in length. As for dramatic verse, it is always mixed with prose in usage. Thus, two of the main genres in Western poetry, epic and tragedy, are practically absent in Chinese. The reasons for this are worth discussing.

The first reason for the lack of epic and tragedy or indeed any other long poem in Chinese is, I think, the nature of the language itself. As we have seen, the language is full of monosyllabic words and disyllabic compounds which, with their fixed tones and *staccato* rhythm, do not lend themselves to long compositions.[1] Moreover, the abundance of homophones also works

---

[1] Cf. above, p. 38.

against poems of great length, for one would soon exhaust all available rimes. A glance at the various verse forms given in Part I, Chapter 3, will show that none of them is suitable for epic or poetic drama unmixed with prose.

Next, the absence of great epics and tragedies each embodying a whole vision of life may also be due to the fluid nature of the Chinese mind. It seems to me the Chinese mind is pragmatic rather than dogmatic: quick in perception and apprehension, it assimilates each experience as it occurs, but does not try to impose a pre-conceived pattern on all experience. The ancient Chinese philosophers such as Confucius and Mencius had a tendency to deal with each problem as it arose, without attempting to formulate comprehensive systems into which all human knowledge and experience could be fitted, as did for instance Aristotle or Kant. As for Chinese poets, most of whom were not great philosophers, they naturally had their philosophical and religious views, but they were more often eclectic than systematic, exhibiting Confucian, Taoist, and Buddhist leanings at the same time, without endeavouring to integrate them into one consistent system. Chinese poets neither used an existing religious and philosophical system as the framework of their poetry, as Dante and Milton did, nor invented their own systems, as Blake did. Tu Fu's extant poetry, which represents but a fraction of what he wrote, reveals as many facets of life, as great a variety of human experience, as profound a reading of human nature, as can be found in any other major poet of the world, yet he never thought it necessary to relate all these to one system of thought in a single work. Critics, too, as we have seen, were liable to be unsystematic. The present writer's obvious tendencies towards systematization and analysis are probably due to his contact with Western culture at an early age, and are in any case encouraged by the fact that he is trying to interpret Chinese poetry to Western readers in terms readily comprehensible to them.

Another trait of the Chinese mind which is in favour of short poems is its concentration on the essence of an object or experience rather than its details. The Chinese poet is usually intent on capturing the spirit of a scene, a mood, a world, rather than depicting its multifarious manifestations. In view of what I said in the last paragraph, the Chinese mentality presents something of a paradox; as far as individual experience is concerned, the

Chinese mind is inclined to concentrate on the essence rather than the appearance, and is therefore 'essentialist'; but in its attitude towards life as a whole, it is more 'existentialist' than 'essentialist' in so far as it concerns itself with actual living experience rather than with Platonic ideas or abstract categories.

One more contributory cause to the absence of epic, or at least heroic epic, in Chinese is the condemnation of the cult of personal valour and physical prowess by Chinese scholars. As Sir Maurice Bowra remarked, 'the great intellectual forces which set so lasting an impress on Chinese civilization were hostile to the heroic spirit with its unfettered individualism and self-assertion.'[1] However, it is only fair to point out that the heroic tradition has not been completely absent in China. During the Warring States period (fifth to third centuries B.C.), knights errant and political assassins played such an important role in contemporary affairs as to warrant the inclusion of their biographies, for the most part sympathetically written, by the great Ssŭ-ma Ch'ien in his monumental *Records of the Historiographer* (*Shih Chi*). Heroes of later periods, especially the warriors of the Three Kingdoms (second to third centuries) and the outlaws at Liangshan at the end of the Northern Sung period (twelfth century) have become household names through popular tales. In fact, the formation of the heroic romance about the Liangshan outlaws, the *Shuei Hu* ('On the Water Margin'), commonly referred to by the misnomer of 'novel', closely resembles that of a heroic epic or saga. It originated from historical events, which, mingled with legends, formed several cycles of tales in an oral tradition. These oral tales were then written down, and after undergoing successive stages of compilation, expansion, and revision by different hands, became the work as we know it to-day. It seems, then, that the heroic tradition was kept among the common people and hence reflected in popular literature, but as it was discouraged by official ideologies, it was excluded from polite letters.[2]

With regard to tragedy, there may be further reasons for its absence in Chinese poetry. The essence of tragedy, as I see it, lies in a view of life which conceives of man's position in the universe as a paradoxical one: human dignity, power, and intelligence on

---

[1] *Heroic Poetry*, p. 14.

[2] Cf. my article 'The Knight Errant in Chinese Literature', *Journal of the Hong Kong Branch of the Royal Asiatic Society*, vol. 1, 1961.

the one hand; human limitations, frailties, and mortality on the other. This tragic sense of life and of man's lot, as I pointed out before, is often present in Chinese poetry, yet it has not been developed into full-fledged tragedy in dramatic form, probably because Chinese poets were reluctant to describe conflict. All the three main ideologies in China were against conflict: Confucianism counselled moderation in all things; Taoism recommended inactivity and submission to Nature; Buddhism preached either total annihilation of consciousness or, in its popular form, retribution through reincarnation. All these doctrines made conflict undesirable or unnecessary, and without conflict tragedy in the Aristotelian sense could not arise. The other ingredients of the Aristotelian conception of tragedy, such as the tragic hero with his *harmatia* and the theory of catharsis, were also alien to Chinese thinking.

Moreover, unlike Greek drama, Chinese drama had a secular origin. It was from first to last a form of entertainment, which developed from singing, dancing, story-telling, buffoonery, and acrobatics. Whether patronized by the court or by a plebeian audience, it had to cater for the mood of people out to have a good time and expecting the fulfilment of poetic justice, the absence of which would have outraged their moral sensibility. Under these circumstances it was more difficult to deal with serious themes and end plays tragically than in the Athens of Pericles. Of course, Shakespeare too had to please a motley audience, but at least the Elizabethan theatre was influenced by mediaeval miracles and mysteries, so that it was easier to write tragedies in such a theatre than in one of purely secular origin and character, like the Chinese.

However, despite the lack of epic and tragedy, Chinese poetry as a whole is not more limited in scope or less profound in thought and feeling than Western poetry. Though we may find it hard to name an *Iliad*, a *Divine Comedy*, an *Oedipus*, or a *Hamlet* in Chinese, the entire body of Chinese poetry presents as rich and varied a panorama of life as any other poetry. While Chinese poetry may fail to compare with Western poetry for magnitude of conception and intensity of emotion, it often surpasses the latter in sensitivity of perception, delicacy of feeling, and subtely of expression. As an exploration of life, it can lead one into worlds unknown or unfamiliar to Western readers; as an exploration of language, it presents a fascinating display of verbal ingenuity and flexibility, with a distinct music which may sound bizarre to Western ears but which has its own charms to those attuned to it. In China, poetry has exerted greater influence on music and painting than in the West, as can be witnessed by the fact that many Chinese songs and pictures are poetic in conception rather than musical or pictorial. It is no exaggeration to claim that Chinese poetry is one of the chief glories of Chinese culture and one of the highest achievements of the Chinese mind.

NOTE ON ROMANIZATION

CHINESE words and names are romanized according to the Wade system as found in *Mathews' Chinese-English Dictionary*, with a few modifications specified below.

The meaningless circumflex above the *e* in *en* and *eng* has been omitted.

The superfluous umlaut mark in *yuan*, *yueh*, and *yun* has been omitted, as there are no syllables with which these can be confused. However, I have retained it in *yü* 俞 to avoid confusion with *yu* 由.

Wade is rather inconsistent in using *uei* for some syllables and *ui* for others which have the same sound (e.g. 歸 is spelt *kuei* but 灰 is spelt *hui*). I have consistently used *uei* where Wade would sometimes give *ui* instead. Thus, I write *tsuei*, *tuei*, etc., instead of *tsui*, *tui*, etc.

In one case I have modified *lien* to *lian* to show it is meant to rime with *shan* (p. 35).

When riming syllables no longer appear as such in modern pronunciation, I have added Karlgren's reconstructed Archaic or Ancient pronunciation, whichever is appropriate, as given in his *Grammata Serica Recensa* (Stockholm, 1957), though I have omitted some of the more subtle phonetic marks. When riming syllables still rime in modern pronunciation, I have not thought it necessary to append the early pronunciation.

In romanizing Chinese names, I have usually given the formal personal names (*ming*) of writers, even if they are referred to by their courtesy names, official titles, etc., in works cited.

REFERENCES

BSS = Basic Sinological Series (*Chien-pien* 簡編)
SPPY = *Ssu Pu Pei Yao* 四部備要
SPTK = *Ssu Pu Ts'ung K'an* (*so-pen* 縮本) 四部叢刊
TSCC = *Ts'ung Shu Chi Ch'eng* 叢書集成
WYWK = *Wan Yu Wen K'u* 萬有文庫
YCH = *Yuan Ch'ü Hsüan* (in SPPY) 元曲選

Page	Line	
11	35	Liu Yü-hsi, *Liu Meng-tê Chi* 劉夢得集 (SPTK), p.66.
12	3	Li Shang-yin, *Li Yi-shan Shih-chi* 李義山詩集 (SPTK), p.36.
22	25	*Mao Shih* 毛詩 (SPTK), p.19.
24	21	Li Po, *Li Tai-po Chi* 李太白集 (BSS), *t'sê* I, p.108.
28	5	Li Shang-yin, *loc.cit.*
29	17	Wang Wei, *Wang Yu-ch'eng Chi Chu* 王右丞集注 (SPPY), *chüan* 14, p.5a.
31	3	*Hua-chien Chi* 花間集 (SPTK), p.9.
32	34	Ma Chih-yuan, *Tung-li Yueh-fu* 東籬樂府 p.116, in *San-ch'ü Ts'ung-k'an* 散曲叢刊
34	21	*Tu Fu Concordance* (Harvard-Yenching Index Series), p.376.
34	29	Po Chü-I, *Po-shih Ch'ang-ch'ing Chi* 白氏長慶集 (SPTK), p.66.
35	9	Tu Fu, *op.cit.*, p.299.
35	18	*Ibid.*, p.422.
35	29	*Ibid.*, p.285.
36	4	*Ibid.*, p.538.
36	28	*Ku Shih Yuan* 古詩源 (BSS), p.53.
37	3	Po Chü-I, *op.cit.*, p.7.
37	10	Ou-yang Hsiu, *Liu-yi Tz'u* 六一詞, p.5a, in *Sung Liu-shih Ming-chia Tz'u* 宋六十名家詞 (SPPY); given as Feng's in *Tz'u Tsung* 詞綜 (SPPY), *chüan* 3, p.7b.
37	21	*Mao Shih*, p.1.
37	24	*Ibid.*, p.7.
37	31	*Wu-t'ung Yü*, p.10b. (YCH, *ping shang* 丙上)
40	13	Wang Wei, *op.cit.*, *chüan* 13, p.2a.
40	37	*Ibid.*, p.4a.
42	11	*Ibid.*, *chüan* 7, p.6b.
43	3	*Loc.cit.*
43	19	Tu Fu, *op.cit.*, p.350.
44	4	*Hua-chien Chi*, p.4.
46	4	Tu Fu, *op.cit.*, p.296.
49	30	T'ao Ch'ien, *T'ao Yuan-ming Chi* 陶淵明集 (SPTK), p.15.
50	29	*Ku Shih Yuan*, p.24.
51	4	*Tz'u Tsung*, *chüan* 25, p.3a.
51	15	*Ch'u Tz'u Chi-chu* 楚辭集注 (facsimile reprint of Yuan edition), *ts'ê* 3, p.93.
52	33	Li Po, *op.cit.*, *ts'ê* 5, p.93.

Page Line
53   25 Wang Wei, *op.cit.*, *chüan* 9, p.2a.
53   27 *Ibid.*, *chüan* 3, p.4a.
53   29 *Ibid.*, *chüan* 7, p.6b.
53   31 *Ibid.*, *chüan* 13, p.2a.
54   15 *Tz'u Tsung*, *chüan* 3, p.7a.
55   30 Li Po, *op.cit.*, *ts'ê* 2, p.91.
56   3   *Hua-chien, Chi*, p.6.
58   7   *Loc.cit.*
59   32 T'ao Ch'ien, *op.cit.*, p.32.
60   2   Li Po, *op.cit.*, *ts'ê* 5, p.114.
65   19 *Analects*, II, 2.
66   1   *Ibid.*, VIII, 8.
66   3   *Ibid.*, XIII, 5.
66   7   *Ibid.*, XVI, 13.
66   9   *Ibid.*, XVII, 9.
66   25 *Mao Shih*, p.1.
66   34 Tu Fu, *op.cit.*, p.2.
66   37 Li Po, *op.cit.*, *ts'ê* 1, p.40.
67   1   Po Chü-I, Letter to Yuan Chen, *op.cit.*, p.142. (partially translated
          in Arthur Waley's *The Life and Times of Po Chü-I*, pp.107-8).
67   10 Shen Tê-ch'ien, *Shuo-shih Ts'uei-yü* 說詩晬語 (SPPY), p.1a.
          Also, Preface to the revised edition of *T'ang-shih Pieh-ts'ai*
          唐詩別裁 p.1. (BSS).
68   9   *Shuo-shih Ts'uei-yü*, p.2b.
68   18 *Ibid.*, p.2a.
68   39 Po Chü-I, Letter to Yuan Chen.
70   10 *Mao Shih*, p.1.
71   3   Liu Hsieh, *Wen-hsin Tiao-lung* (with notes by Huang Shu-lin,
          supplementary notes by Li Hsiang, further supplements by
          Yang Ming-chao, Shanghai, 1958), p.34.
71   22 *Loc.cit.*
71   32 *Ibid.*, pp.216-7.
73   25 Chin Sheng-t'an, Letter to Chin Wen-ch'ang, in *Chin-tai San-wen
          Ch'ao* 近代散文抄 (edited by Shen Ch'i-wu, reprinted Hong
          Kong, 1957), p.290.
73   36 Yuan Mei, *Sui-yuan Shih-hua* 隨園詩話, Supplement *chüan* 1, p.1a
          (in *Sui-yuan San-shih-liu Chung* 隨園三十六種).
74   10 *Ibid.*, *chüan* 3, p.4a.
74   23 Chin Sheng-t'an, Letter to Hsü Ch'ing-hsü, *op.cit.*, p.292.
75   9   Yuan Mei, *op.cit.*, *chüan* 1, p.2a.
75   16 Chin Sheng-t'an, Letter to Shen K'uang-lai, *op.cit.*, p.294.
75   28 Yuan Mei, *op.cit.*, *chüan* 3, p.3b.
75   36 *Ibid.*, p.6b.
76   2   *Ibid.*, *chüan* 1, p.8b.
78   26 Quoted in Monk Huei-hung's *Leng-chai Yeh-hua* 冷齋夜話
          (TSCC), p.5.

Page Line

78 31 *Loc.cit.*

79 3 Li Tung-yang, *Huai-lu-t'ang Shih-hua,* quoted in Kuo Shao-yü's
        Chung-kuo Wen-hsueh-p'i-p'ing Shih 中國文學批評史
        (2nd edition, 1948), vol.2, p.173.

79 7 *Loc.cit.*

79 11 *Ibid.,* p.175.

79 19 *Tu-shih Shuang-sheng Tieh-yun P'u* 杜詩雙聲疊韻譜 (TSCC), *passim.*

79 27 Kuo Shao-yü, *op.cit.,* p.186.

79 37 Li Meng-yang, *K'ung-t'ung Chi* 空同集, *chüan* 61, pp.11b-12a.
        Quoted in Kuo, *op.cit.,* p.187.

80 17 Weng Fang-kang, *Fu-ch'u-chai Wen-chi* 復初齋文集, *chüan* 8, p.1a-b.
        Quoted in Kuo, *op.cit.,* p.633.

80 35 *Ibid.,* p.9a-b.

81 20 Yen Yü, *Ts'ang-lang Shih-hua* 滄浪詩話 (with notes by Hu Chien)
        chüan 1, p.6a.

82 9 *Ibid.,* p.6b.

82 22 *Ibid.,* p.6a.

82 26 *Loc.cit.*

83 6 Wang Fu-chih, *Hsi-t'ang Yung-jih Hsü-lun* 夕堂永日緒論 p.4b,
        in *Wang Ch'uan-shan Yi-shu* 王船山遺書

83 11 Wang Fu-chih, *Shih Yi* 詩譯, p.5b, in *Wang Ch'uan-shan Yi-shu.*

83 15 *Hsi-t'ang Yung-jih Hsü-lun,* p.9a.

83 36 *Po-shih Shih-shuo* 白石詩說, quoted in *Yü-yang Shih-hua* 漁洋詩話
        (Shanghai, 1928 reprint), *chüan,* 1, p.8b.

84 3 Wang Shih-chen, *Ts'an-wei Wen* 蠶尾文, *chüan* 1, p.13b, in
        Tai-ching-t'ang Chi 帶經堂集

84 24 Wang Kuo-wei, *Jen-chien Tz'u-hua* 人間詞話 (with notes by
        Hsü T'iao-fu, Peking, 1955), p.3.

84 33 *Ibid.,* p.1.

85 8 Yen Yü, *op.cit., chüan* 1, p.1a-b.

85 18 Wang Fu-chih, *loc.cit.*

85 22 Wang Shih-chen, *Tai-ching-t'ang Shih-hua, chüan.* 3, p.8a.

85 27 *Ibid.,* p.9b-p.10a. Or *Yü-yang Shih-hua, loc.cit.*

86 5 Yen Yü, *op.cit., chüan* 1, p.6a.

86 21 Wang Kuo-wei, *op.cit.,* p.21.

86 22 Yen Yü, *loc.cit.*

86 32 Wang Shih-chen, *Ch'ih-pei Ou-t'an* 池北偶談 (Shanghai, Commercial
        Press reprint), p.209. Or *Tai-ching-t'ang Shih-hua, chüan* 3, p.2b.

97 23 Ku Yen-wu, *Jih-chih Lu* 日知錄 (WYWK), vol.7, p.70.

97 30 Wang Kuo-wei, *op.cit.,* p.37.

99 24 *Tz'u Tsung, chüan* 2, p.2a.

105 29 *Shih-ching T'ung-yi* 詩經通義, in *Wen I-to Ch'üan-chi,* 聞一多全集
        vol.2, pp.192-3.

106 11 Yü P'ing-po, *Tu Shih Cha-chi* 讀詩札記, p.212.

107 12 *Mao Shih,* p.5.

107 31 Tu Fu, *op.cit.,* p.280.

108 17 See p.31

Page	Line	
108	19	*Hua-chien Chi*, p.1.
108	21	See p.128
109	9	*Tz'u Tsung, chüan* 2, p.1b.
109	19	Tu Fu, *op.cit.*, p.507.
110	7	*Hua-chien Chi*, p.1.
111	25	*Tz'u Tsung, chüan* 1, p.2b.
111	31	*Ibid.*, p.7b.
112	11	Li Shang-yin, *op.cit.*, p.47.
113	4	*Wen Hsüan* 文選 (SPTK), p.419.
113	30	Chia Tao, *Ch'ang-chiang Chi* 長江集 (SPTK), p.12.
114	7	Han Yü, *Ch'ang-li Hsien-sheng Chi* 昌黎先生集 (SPTK), pp.24, 55.
114	15	Meng Chiao, *Meng Tung-yeh Shih-chi* 孟東野詩集 (SPTK), p.9.
116	1	Wang An-shih, *Lin-ch'uan Hsien-sheng Wen-chi* 臨川先生文集 (SPTK), p.64.
116	30	Su Shih, *Tung-p'o Hou-chi* 東坡後集 (SPPY), *chüan* 2, p.2b.
116	35	*Chin-ch'ien Chi*, p.8b. (YCH, *chia shang* 甲上).
117	4	*Loc.cit.*
117	7	*Tz'u Tsung, chüan* 25, p.2b.
117	13	*Ch'iang-t'ou Ma-shang*, p.2a. (YCH, *yi hsia* 乙下)
117	30	*Chou Mei-hsiang*, p.4b. (YCH, *keng hsia* 庚下)
118	15	*Wu-t'ung Yü*, p.10b. (YCH, *ping shang* 丙上)
119	20	*Han Kung Ch'iu*, p.5b. (YCH, *chia shang* 甲上)
119	30	*Chin-hsien Ch'ih*, p.4a. (YCH, *hsin shang* 辛上)
120	12	*Hsi-hsiang Chi* (with notes by Ch'en Chih-hsien, Shanghai, 1948), Part IV, p.37.
120	28	*Ch'ien-nü Li-hun*, p.6a. (YCH, *wu shang* 戊上)
121	16	*Ch'ing-shan Lei*, p.1b. (YCH, *chi hsia* 己下)
121	24	*Hsieh T'ien-hsiang*, p.1b. (YCH, *chia hsia* 甲下)
122	8	*Hsi-hsiang Chi*, Part IV, p.44.
122	14	*Wu-t'ung Yü*, p.8a.
122	18	*Ibid.*, p.9b.
123	15	Li Po, *op.cit.*, *ts'ê* 2, p.80.
123	25	Tu Fu, *op.cit.*, p.278.
124	3	Wang Wei, *op.cit.*, *chüan* 8, p.10b.
124	7	Li Po, *op.cit.*, *ts'e* 4, p.65.
124	12	Tu Fu, *op.cit.*, p.415.
125	10	Kao Shih, *Kao Ch'ang-shih Chi* 高常侍集 (SPTK), p.42.
125	14	Meng Chiao, *op.cit.*, p.23.
125	17	Wang Kuo-wei, *op.cit.*, p.33.
125	33	*Analects*, IX, 27.
126	8	Tu Fu, *op.cit.*, p.277.
126	29	*Ibid.*, pp.276-7.
128	3	*Hua-chien Chi*, p.1.
128	36	*Ch'u Tz'u Chi-chu*, *ts'ê* 1, p.7b.
129	17	T'ao Ch'ien, *op.cit.*, p.31.
129	25	Wang An-shih, *op.cit.*, p.95.

129   35   *Tz'u Tsung, chüan* 25, p.3b.

130   2   *Ibid.*, p.3a.

132   31   Tu Fu, *op.cit.*, p.472.

133   20   *Ibid.*, p.296.

133   38   *Ch'ien-nü Li-hun*, p.5a.

134   7   *Ibid.*, p.5b.

134   30   *Hsi-hsiang Chi*, Part IV, p.54.

134   36   *Han Kung Ch'iu*, p.7b.

135   11   *Chou Mei-hsiang*, p.11b.

135   20   The story is given in *Ch'ing Shih* 情史 (1806). For Zoroastrianism
            see Chang Hsing-lang, *Chung-hsi Chiao-t'ung Shih-liao Huei-
            pien* 中西交通史料滙編 (Peking, 1930), vol.4, pp.122-34.

135   33   Wang Kuo-wei, *Ch'ü Lu* 曲 錄, *chüan* 2, p.11, in *Wang Ching-an
            Hsien-sheng Yi-shu.* 王靜安先生遺書

136   22   Li Shang-yin, *op.cit.*, p.45.

136   35   *Ibid.*, p.33.

137   8   *Ibid.*, p.58.

139   3   *Ibid.*, p.41.

139   24   *Ku Shih Yuan*, p.31.

139   37   *Yueh-fu Shih-chi* 樂府 詩集 (SPTK), p.353.

140   9   *Wen Hsüan*, p.293.

140   21   *Yueh-fu Shih-chi*, p.364.

140   30   *Ku Shih Yuan*, p.75.

141   29   *Analects*, VII, 5; Hsin Ch'i-chi, *Chia-hsüan Tz'u* 稼軒 詞, *chüan* 1,
            p.6a, in *Sung Liu-shih Ming-chia Tz'u.*

142   6   Tu Fu, *op.cit.*, p.308; *Li Ku'ei Fu-ching*, p.2a. (YCH, *jen hsia* 壬下)

142   8   Tu Fu, *op.cit.*, p.307; *Chin-hsien Ch'ih*, p.3a.

142   27   *Chou Mei-hsiang*, p.9a.

143   11   *Han Kung Ch'iu*, p.1b.

143   21   *Chou Mei-hsiang*, p.9a.

143   37   *Ibid.*, p.2a.

144   10   Li T'iao-yuan, *Yü-ts'un Ch'ü-hua* 雨村曲話 , *chüan* 1, p.11a;
            Liang T'ing-nan, *Ch'ü-hua*, *chüan* 2, p.6b. (Both reprinted in
            Ch'ü Yuan 曲 苑, 1921).

147   26   Li Po, *op.cit.*, *ts'ê* 1, p.48.

148   7   Wang Po, *Wang Tzu-an Chi* 王子安集 (SPTK), p.34.

148   15   Wang Wei, *op.cit.*, *chüan* 7, p.6b.

148   26   See p.43

149   3   See p.124

149   11   Tu Fu, *op.cit.*, p.296.

149   34   *Tz'u Tsung, chüan* 4, p.4a.

150   9   *Han Kung Ch'iu*, p.2a.

150   16   *Ibid.*, p.86.

150   23   *Li K'uei Fu-ching*, p.2a.

Note: Names and titles that appear only in the list of references but not in the text are not included in this index.